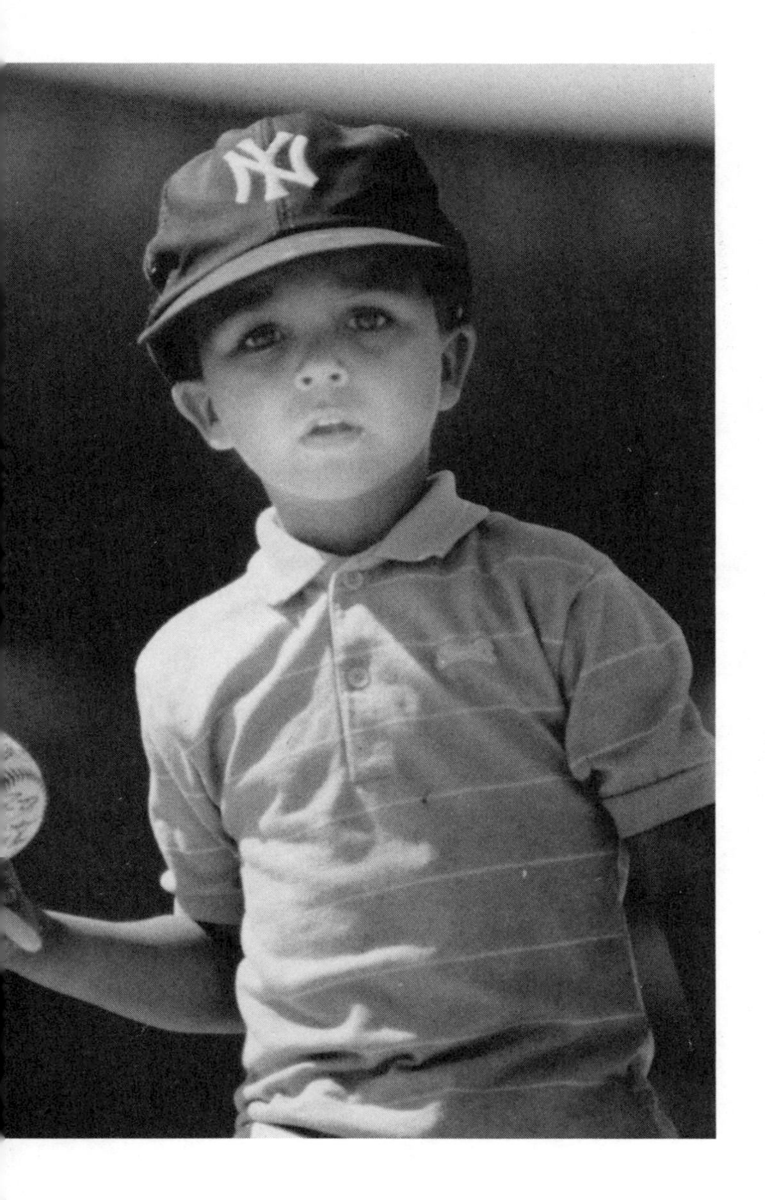

The Traveler's Guide to Baseball Spring Training

1991 Edition

The Traveler's Guide to Baseball Spring Training

1991 Edition

John Garrity

Andrews and McMeel
A Universal Press Syndicate Company
Kansas City/New York

To Ron Tankel, who loves spring training more than anybody, but doesn't get to go.

"Quoting from Scripture," first appeared in *Sports Illustrated.*

"In the Heat of the Day," first appeared in *City* magazine.

Library of Congress Cataloging-in-Publication Data

Garrity, John
The traveler's guide to baseball spring training / John Garrity.—Rev.
p. cm.
ISBN 0-8362-7982-4 : $9.95
1. Baseball—Florida—Training—Miscellanea. 2. Florida—Description and travel—1981- —Guide-books. 3. Baseball—Arizona—Training—Miscellanea. 4. Arizona—Description and travel—1981- —Guide-books. 5. Baseball—United States—Clubs—Miscellanea. I. Title.
GV875.6.G37 1990 90-47822
796.357'64'0973—dc20 CIP

Attention: Schools and Businesses

Andrews and McMeel books are available at quantity discounts for bulk purchase for educational, business, or sales promotional use. For information, please write to: Special Sales Department, Andrews and McMeel, 4900 Main Street, Kansas City, Missouri 64112.

Contents

Grapefruit League

Cactus League

NO
TRYOUTS
DURING
SPRING
TRAINING

Introduction

Baseball has always cloaked itself in the annual symbolism of spring, never realizing what a fabulous, accidental marketing gimmick this actually was. Now we are forced to realize that it wasn't baseball that made us feel so wonderful at this time of year. It was simply the end of winter that made our spirits explode and our hopes rise.

—Tom Boswell

I won't dwell on the spring training lockout of 1989, but the reader will understand that I took it personally. I remember driving a rental car somewhere last March, the radio turned to a sports talk show, when a caller threw out that tired cliché: "Hey, Biff, it's not the owners and players who are getting hurt by the lockout—it's the fans."

I nearly ran off the road.

"Bull——!" I cried. "I'll tell you who's getting hurt. It's the authors of spring-training travel guides!"

You see, when there is no spring baseball, there is no need for the quaint volume you hold in your hands. That makes me one of the principal victims of the '89 lockout, if not the most publicized. One newspaper wrote, "I hope Andrews and McMeel didn't print too many copies of Garrity's book."

Well, they did. *The Traveler's Guide to Baseball Spring Training* peaked at number 2,754 on the *New York Times* best-seller list.

It's only now, as I prepare the 1990 edition, that I see the bright side of this debacle; since practically nobody read the 1989 edition, I don't have to write much new material.

And that's why, if you possess last year's guide (now a collector's item), you will find the 1990 edition to be—in Yogi Berra's memorable phrase—"*déjà vu* all over again." Same interviews, same features, same essays. Everything that could be salvaged, was.

Even so, this edition is as fresh and up-to-date as printing deadlines will allow. New essays accompany those teams that have moved or seen significant changes in their camps—most notably the Twins, the Orioles, and the Royals. The travel and entertainment sections have been updated, ticket prices and addresses made current, and all photographs and references to Pete Rose removed.

Let's forget about the lockout, then, and pretend the Silent Spring never happened. Here, unabridged and unexpurgated, is the original introduction to *The Traveler's Guide to Baseball Spring Training:*

In the beginning, I didn't go to spring training; spring training came to me. I learned my multiplication tables at Central Elementary School in West Palm Beach, Florida, on a hill overlooking a ballpark. The ballpark was Connie Mack Stadium, spring training home of the Philadelphia/Kansas City Athletics. I still possess, tucked away in a trunk, a baseball-clinic diploma signed by certain major-leaguers attesting to my mastery of fundamental baseball skills. (The A's put a few dozen of us awed schoolboys through a regular spring-training workout one hot Saturday morning, complete with calisthenics, batting and fielding practice, and hook-sliding lessons at the sliding pit.) Once I even stood before Connie Mack himself, who by then was a milky-eyed cadaver with a tie knotted tight around a ropey throat. I said, "Nice to meet you, sir," and got away fast.

The Palm Beach County school system had a nice tradition: Each pupil could skip class one afternoon each spring to attend an exhibition baseball game. A parental note was required, but there were no other conditions. You would have thought, though, that the school board had specified a Yankee or Dodgers game, because those were the only two teams my classmates wanted to see. Four-fifths of my classmates were Yankee fans, classic front-runners who wore you out with Mickey Mantle, Hank Bauer, Whitey Ford, and the lovable Yogi. The other fifth, proudly defiant, rooted for the Dodgers . . . never mind that none of them knew exactly where or what Brooklyn was. The arguments were shrill and endless. They sometimes ended with a bloody nose; more often they ended with a game of baseball at nearby Howard Park.

Even as children, we recognized the essential truth about exhibition games: They don't count. We watched them fitfully, preferring to race around after foul balls, hound players for autographs, and scavenge for treasure under the bleacher seats. Being local kids, we had no adult supervision. That, as much as any innate love for the National Pastime, explained why we went to the ballpark: to run amok.

Still, the spring game left lasting impressions. The first time I saw the Pirates' Smoky Burgess with that huge wad of chewing tobacco in his cheek, I thought it was a goiter. Gus Zernial, the White Sox slugger, set a standard of outfield play by which I measure players to this day (usually favorably). And I'm not likely to forget those noble members of the Yankees who saluted a small band of us clamoring for autographs by opening the windows of the team bus and spitting on us. Kids survive such disillusionments, and childhood slights are best judged by their storytelling potential. Over the years, having told of my trial by saliva at least a hundred times, I feel I got off with a bargain. I smile when present-day autograph hounds tell me that the Yanks are "jerks" and "the pits of the autograph world."

As a grown man, I returned to Florida to write about baseball, and that's when I learned what it meant to "go" to spring training. Oddly enough, the games themselves held my attention no better than they had when I was four feet tall. In ten years of watching the Royals play at Ft. Myers, Florida, I never made it past the sixth inning, and I was invariably mistreating a golf ball at Lochmoore Country Club by the time Dan Quisenberry or some lesser light got the last out in the ninth. For this reason, I am suspicious of writers who extol the virtues of spring baseball without mentioning stone crabs, palm trees, and one's inalienable right to work in shorts. At least one of my colleagues agrees. "Too much . . . is written about the idyllic charms and optimism of spring training," writes Scott Ostler of *The National.* "The two main topics in any spring baseball camp are: a) last night's dinner, and b) tonight's dinner."

Which brings me, the long way around, to this book, *The Traveler's Guide to Baseball Spring Training.* The idea of a spring-training guide is not original. Every newspaper big enough to send a reporter to Florida or Arizona, plus every newspaper *in* Florida and Arizona, runs a spread every spring with maps and stadium facts and ticket information. Most of this data comes from a handy volume called *The Official Cactus and Grapefruit League Media Guide*, put out yearly by the Major League Baseball news department. The reader will understand that this writer has no more love for library carrels than the next fellow, and that most of the statistical data in this book—won/lost records, attendance figures, former spring-training sites—was copied directly from the media guide. Any errors are the sole responsibility of Susan Aglietti and Craig Barbarino of the MLB news department.

As for the travel guide aspects of this volume, I need to make a few disclaimers. First of all, I am no restaurant critic. My favorite place to eat in Florida is Morrison's Cafeteria, and I always get the fried shrimp. Not usually, *always.* By my estimate, I have gone through Morrison's lines two hundred or so times without once falling for the grilled chicken teriyaki or the broiled red snapper with lemon and butter. Therefore, I freely admit that I am unprepared to judge the sauteed eel at your finer hash houses. All the restaurant recommendations in this book come from baseball people who were asked where *they* liked to eat. Their taste may be abominable, but it's bound to be better than mine.

Disclaimer Number Two: *Don't blame me if you get lost.* I have taken great care to make sure that my stadium directions are accurate, but written directions have a way of turning ambiguous when you get behind the wheel of a car. For instance, the directions to St. Petersburg's Al Lang Stadium say to get off I-295 at Exit 9 and follow the signs to the stadium. Well, spring before last there were no signs to the stadium, and I got lost every time. (St. Pete is one of those places where the avenues and streets are numbered the same and tagged N.W., S.W., N.E., S.E., thereby greatly increasing the chance that the address you're looking for is twelve miles in the opposite direction.) It's always a good idea to carry a map; it makes a nice prop when you stop at a gas station to ask for directions.

Disclaimer Number Three: *I am not responsible if you can't get tickets.* I can't stress this enough. The soaring popularity of the spring game has created a ticket crisis for some clubs. Fans camp outside HoHoKam Park in Mesa, Arizona, before sunrise to be at the front of the line for general admission tickets, and Cubs games are invariably sold out. The Texas Rangers draw big crowds to Port Charlotte, Florida, the Toronto Blue Jays sell out tiny Grant Field with regularity, and the New York Mets went so far one March as to issue a press release threatening to prosecute ticket scalpers. If you are planning a trip around spring baseball, order your tickets early to avoid disappointment.

Disclaimer Number Four: *Things change.* The phone numbers, theme park prices, parking fees, etc., were as accurate as I could make them when this book went to press. Prices, especially, can and do change without notice.

Finally, I must disclose to the reader my definition of "charm," that most overused word to describe a good spring-training park. To me, as to most curmudgeons, charm means small, not large; old, not new; intimate, not grand. I deplore fenced-off player parking and tunnels that separate the players from the fans. I like wood and steel stadiums, not concrete ones. And I prefer grass to synthetic turf. Knowing my prejudices, you can easily adjust for your own definition of charm.

Of course, in the immortal words of radio's Pete Franklin, "You could argue, but you'd be wrong."

Acknowledgments: The author would like to especially thank Teresa Woodrum, who printed most of the photographs in this book; John Hendel of UPI, for his invaluable assistance and his Tibetan monk impression; Alan Eskew of the *Topeka Capital Journal,* for reporting assistance and use of his Winter Haven condo; and Bill Althaus of the *Independence Examiner,* for his research help. I am, of course, indebted to Craig Barbarino and Susan Aglietti of the Major League Baseball News Department, and to all twenty-six major league public relations directors and their staffs.

Grapefruit League

WELCOME TO
Dodgertown

STADIUM INFORMATION

Holman Stadium
4101 26th St.
Vero Beach, FL 32961-2887
(407) 569-4900

How long at present location: Forty-two years
Capacity: 6,500 plus outfield grass seating
Dimensions: 340 feet down lines; 410 feet to center
Directions: Exit I-95 at Vero Beach; take Route 60 east to 43rd Ave., turn left; Dodgertown entrance is straight ahead—turn right on 26th St. First right is golf course, second right is stadium.
Parking: Mostly grass and dispersed along fairways and under trees in Dodgertown. Free.

"I've never been a big fan of Vero Beach," says *Washington Post* baseball writer Tom Boswell. "It's always been too perfect for me."

That's a backhanded way of saying that Dodgertown is still unsurpassed as a spring-training facility. "It's charming," a TV reporter said last spring after visiting the late Walter O'Malley's 450-acre baseball resort for the first time. "It has all those little touches that are so corny that they're perfect."

He obviously meant the outdoor globe lamps painted to look like baseballs . . . the rest-room doors designated "Bat Boys" and "Bat Girls" . . . or perhaps the sign beside a birdbath-size pond O'Malley put in some years back: DODGER LAKE—NO SURFING, SAILING OR WATER SKIING. Whimsy and nostalgia reign at Dodgertown.

And tradition. Even a lifetime Dodger-hater, standing at the junction of Roy Campanella and Sandy Koufax Drives, feels the tug of tradition. Players crunch by in their spiked shoes as they make baseball's most wonderful walk—the after-game hike from Holman Stadium to the Dodgers clubhouse, a quarter-mile away—across green practice fields streaked with sunlight and unhurried shadows. Cambridge at dusk, with gowned dons bicycling by and lovers punting on the Cam, is no greater wonder than Dodgertown as it winds down in the evening (especially when manager Tom Lasorda scoots by in his golf cart, a Dodger-blue Mr. Chips hurrying to tea).

It's all so perfect that one wonders why more ballclubs haven't copied Dodgertown instead of cluttering the Florida peninsula with their penally-inspired encampments. Here are a few of the Holman Stadium touches that other clubs should consider adapting:

• **No dugouts.** The players sit in shallow trenches in the hot sun; live fans breathe down their necks. Such intimacy improves the fans' manners and discourages player snobbery.

• **No outfield wall.** Well, there's a Little-League-size chain-link fence. A grassy berm contains the outfield and provides a home-run target. Spectators sit on the grass when the park is sold out, which is often.

• **No music from MTV.** The taste of the Holman Stadium disk jockey leans toward John Philip Sousa and Stephen Foster, with occasional forays into the more radical works of Les Paul and Mary Ford.

But no, Tom, Dodgertown isn't perfect. If it were, they'd allow water-skiing on Dodger Lake.

55

Ticket Information: reserved $7, standing room $4 (1990 prices). Tickets may be purchased at the box office or by writing Los Angeles Dodgers, Attn. Ticket Office, P.O. Box 2887, Vero Beach, FL 32961-2887. Telephone orders are not accepted; MasterCard and VISA are not accepted.

Autograph Opportunities: "Dodgertown is my favorite place," says collector Tom Bunevich of Tampa, "because the Dodgers intentionally allow a lot of contact with the players." The Dodgers clubhouse is way, way east of the ballpark, and players stroll back and forth all day long, using the same walks and paths as the fans. On some of the practice fields, only a golf-tournament-style rope separates the players from the fans.

"The Dodgers are easy and accessible," says Greg Hileman, a collector from Winter Haven, "but Eddie Murray is almost impossible. Kirk Gibson is a moody player; he usually signs only in the afternoon." Says Bunevich: "The problem is, the crowds picked up after the championship season. We went over on Easter Sunday and waited for the players to come in, but most of them gave us the cold shoulder. Gibson signed for us, though, which was a shock."

The stadium is also good hunting, since the players have no dugout to hide in. The railing down the right-field line is especially good for visiting-team signatures.

Hotels: There is no team hotel, and Dodgertown lodging is closed to the public during spring training. Unmarried Dodgers and minor-leaguers double up in Dodgertown's ninety sleeping rooms. The club sentences Dodgers with families to hotels and condominiums on the beach.

Among the ocean-view hotels in Vero Beach, the most interesting is the Driftwood Inn, a look-what-you-can-build-with-stuff-you-found-on-the-beach sort of place decorated in Shipwreck Modern. Also on the beach are the Holiday Inn Oceanside, the Pickett Suite Hotel, Days Inn, and the Best Western Vero Beach Inn (formerly the Sheraton), where several of the Dodgers stay. Various chain motels are located on the mainland as well.

Area Attractions

• **Golf.** You can't stay at Dodgertown during spring training, but both golf courses are open to the public. For tee times at the eighteen-hole Dodger Pines Country Club, call (407) 569-4400. For the nine-hole Dodgertown Golf Club, call (407) 569-4800. (The ballplayers, who play for free, aren't allowed to tee off until after 3 P.M.)
• **Beaches.** The locals prefer South Beach, which is a big stretch of sand and water with some good restaurants nearby, but not much else. For beaches that are closer to shopping and the hotels, work your way north to Huminston Beach, Conn Beach, and Jaycee Beach.

Restaurants, Lounges, and Dives: The Dodgers' assessment of the local night life is neatly summed up by their nickname for the town: "Zero Beach." Former Dodger third baseman Bill Madlock once complained, "They even play country music in the *discos* here."

"The only restaurant in the old days was the Ocean Grill, which was better known as the 'Bucket of Blood,' " says *Los Angeles Times* sports columnist Jim Murray. "I usually eat at the base now (Dodgertown)." Another great columnist, *The National*'s Scott Ostler, ate at the Ocean Grill more recently and found it excellent. "It's right on the water and has a real funky atmosphere, and they have conchs for appetizers—my wife remembers that; I don't. I had the salmon, and it was very good. The other real good place we ate was an Italian restaurant called Nino's, which is in a mini-mall on the other side of the big bridge when you're leaving the seashore. It's nothing fancy, but the food was outstanding."

Because it's convenient and the food is good, Dodgertown residents eat many of their meals

"I was a victim of a classic prank at Dodgertown four or five years ago. I walked into the clubhouse one day, and Rick Monday and Tom Lasorda were screaming at each other—'He can!' . . . 'He can't!' . . . 'Five hundred dollars says he can!' . . . 'Five hundred dollars says he can't!'

"I got pulled into it. They told me that Jerry Reuss had studied yoga over the summer and claimed he could lift 600 pounds. 'That's two 300-pound guys!'

"Someone said, 'How much do you weigh, Dick?'

"I said 205, and they said, 'That's perfect, we'll get three guys.'

"The whole team is screaming and yelling, and before I know it, I'm lying on the floor with Rick Monday on one side and Steve Yeager on the other. We lock our arms and legs. And that's when it dawns on me: I'm defenseless and immobile. I *know* something is gonna go wrong.

"So Reuss comes out and starts his yoga number—'Please respect me, I must have total silence!'—then he bends over, undoes my belt, pulls down my pants, and pours all this stuff in my crotch—mustard, relish, ketchup, mayonnaise. I was totally helpless. All I could do was laugh.

"Afterwards, they were real nice, putting my clothes through the laundry and sending me off neat as a pin. I said, 'Boy, I must really be dumb to fall for something like that.'

"They said, 'That's nothing, we had one guy who fell for it *twice*.' "

—Dick Schaap, author and
ABC-TV sports commentator

in the private Dodgertown dining room, which is as elegantly appointed as most hotel restaurants.

Chamber of Commerce: 1216 21st St., P.O. Box 2947, Vero Beach, FL 32960; (407) 567-3491.

Spring Training Sites: 1901, Charlotte, NC; 1902–06, Columbia, SC; 1907–09, Jacksonville, FL; 1910–12, Hot Springs, AR; 1913–14, Augusta, GA; 1915–16, Daytona Beach, FL; 1917–18, Hot Springs, AR; 1919–20, Jacksonville, FL; 1921, New Orleans; 1922, Jacksonville, FL; 1923–32, Clearwater, FL; 1933, Miami; 1934–35, Orlando; 1936–40, Clearwater, FL; 1941–42, Havana, Cuba; 1943–45, Bear Mountain, NY; 1946, Daytona Beach, FL; 1947, Havana, Cuba;1948, Cuidad Trujillo, DR; 1949–present, Vero Beach, FL.

Won–Lost Record/Attendance:

Year	Record	Attendance
1989	16–16	78,903
1988	21–11	72,899
1987	12–14	72,491
1986	12–16–1	84,428
1985	16–11	70,993

An Interview with Dodgertown Managing Director Craig Callan

Q: What is Dodgertown exactly?
A: Dodgertown is a 450-acre baseball facility and conference center owned by the Los Angeles Dodgers. In addition to Holman Stadium, we have three full baseball fields, two half practice fields, ninety sleeping rooms, two golf courses, a recreation room, a dining room, twelve executive meeting rooms, forty-five homes in Safari Pines Estates, seventy acres of citrus groves . . . I could go on. We have our own Vero Beach Dodgers, who play a 140-game schedule in the Florida State League. The New Orleans Saints trained here for ten years, and we still average two weeks a year of NFL teams. They utilize Dodgertown during post-season play. The Cleveland Browns, the New England Patriots, the Green Bay Packers—if they're going to be playing in a warm-weather environment, they come down and use our facilities.

Q: The property used to be an air base?
A: That's right. During the war, this was a naval air base for night fighter planes. After the war, a Vero Beach businessman named Bud Holman—whom the stadium is named for—contacted the Dodgers and asked if they would be interested in utilizing the airport property, which had a bunch of old barracks on it. We had been training in St. Pete, Daytona, the Dominican Republic, all over. The deal was, "Come down and you can lease the property for a dollar a year plus the proceeds of one game."

Q: They say that Bobby Bragan got his first look at Dodgertown and said, "Where's the barbed wire and dogs?"
A: Yeah, the old-timers tell stories about how cold it used to be in the barracks and how tough the training was. It was wood floors, no insulation—sort of like basic training. The Dodger farm teams came here in 1948 and the Dodgers the year after. They were the first team to train with their minor-leaguers. At that time, Vero Beach's population was 3,000, and we brought down 600 players. The Dodgers had twenty-six farm teams, so you can imagine the impact on Vero Beach. There were so many players, in fact, that in addition to numbers they had to have different-colored uniforms.

Q: The Dodgers no longer lease the land?
A: No. In 1965, Walter O'Malley purchased the

SNIDER STREET
VIN SCULLY WAY

first 110 acres, which became the conference center and the Dodgertown nine-hole golf club. Today we employ about 200 people on a year-round basis. We're open for groups when the Dodgers aren't here. We also have three baseball fantasy camps for adults. The first one is in November. We bring in 15 Dodger greats from the past, and people pay $3,895 to come down and play baseball and get instruction. There's another camp the week before spring training, and the week before that we have an Ultimate Fantasy Baseball Camp, where every instructor is a Hall of Famer, not necessarily a Dodger.

Q: Who lives at Dodgertown?
A: The minor leaguers, mostly. Every June, after the baseball draft, we bring in all the newly drafted players for a week or so before they're assigned to half-season teams. We work them out and train them on the same fields that Sandy Koufax and Don Drysdale worked out on. They get exposed to all that Dodger history, which is great.

The rest of the year, we arrange a lot of things for the players who are here. We have a recreation hall with pool tables and Ping-Pong tables; we have nightly movies; we give out VIP cards so they can play golf after they practice. We have educational things, too—speakers who come in and talk about nutrition, finances, what-have-you. At Christmas we have a big party for about 400 people. Santa Claus comes, all the children get presents, we rent rides from a carnival and get a ton of snow from an ice house.

During spring training we have about one theme party a week, to break up the monotony. The St. Patrick's Day party is the biggest, the O'Malleys being Irish and all. There's also a big western barbecue for all the players and their families.

Q: Anything new in development?
A: We've built four indoor batting tunnels so the players won't have to miss their hitting during bad weather. They're lighted at 100 foot-candles, about the same as the lighting for a night game. They can be used day or night.

Q: Who should people contact if they want to bring a group to Dodgertown?
A: They should call (407) 569-4900 and ask for the sales department.

STADIUM INFORMATION

St. Lucie County Stadium
525 N.W. Peacock Blvd.
Port St. Lucie, FL 34986
(407) 871-2100

How long at present location: Three years
Capacity: 7,347
Dimensions: 338 feet down lines; 410 feet to center
Directions: From I-95, take exit 63B, follow signs to stadium. From Florida Turnpike, take Exit 54, Port St. Lucie. After toll, make very sharp left onto Bayshore Blvd., go north approximately two miles; turn left onto Prima Vista Blvd., go two miles to Peacock Loop and turn right. Complex is on right. From U.S. 1, take Prima Vista Blvd. west two miles past Bay Shore Blvd. to the Loop, turn right.
Parking: Plentiful, on grass.

St. Lucie County Stadium is what you get when a real estate deal, not baseball considerations, motivates a move to a new spring-training site. Let's talk gigantism: a hulking concrete stadium with concrete-walled ramps, a massive concrete roof, a culvertlike press box so high up it interferes with commercial air traffic, all surrounded by a vast, car-choked parking lot carved out of the pine woods. The only difference between a Mets game here and a regular-season Mets game is that grimy old Shea Stadium is more intimate and more fun—drunks and all.

Everyone connected with this Utopia in the Pines says that St. Lucie West will be a stunning development. The master plan for the 4,600-acre project promises homes, an office park, shopping centers, golf courses, a regional mall, universities (note the plural), and a medical complex. Naturally, they built the stadium first, and the vocabulary of the moves that made it possible is replete with high-dollar coinages such as "income stream" and "two-cent tourist tax surcharge." According to a press kit distributed by the Mets, "Thomas J. White offered to donate 100 acres of land, free and clear, and to construct the stadium facilities, if the county would assign to him the proceeds of the tourist tax for the next fifteen years. In that way, private industry took the risk, St. Lucie County got the sports complex officials wanted, and the New York Mets got the finest spring-training baseball facility in existence."

Thomas J. White, of course, is the developer of the remaining 4,500 acres.

The baseball complex, taken as a whole, *is* impressive: six-and-a-half fields, a 16,000-square-foot minor-league facility, all the modern amenities. But the stadium—the summer home of the St. Lucie Mets of the Florida State League—is devoid of charm and seems designed to keep spectators as far away from the players as possible. "The fan has definitely been left out of the equation," says *Sports Illustrated*'s Ron Fimrite.

Advice to Mets fans: Don't go. Catch your heroes when they play up the road at Dodgertown.

Ticket Information: At press time, the Mets had not yet released their 1991 ticket information. For ticket information, call (407) 871-2115. In 1989, box seats to all home games sold out

17
REYES
15

early; only $4 bleacher tickets were sold at the ticket office.

Autograph Opportunities: Bob McMackin, owner of Bob's Baseball Cards in Port St. Lucie, says that sales of baseballs, 8-by-10-inch photos, and team sets fell off two years ago when people found out how hard it was to get autographs at St. Lucie County Stadium. "It's a very hard ballpark," says McMackin. "It's been called everything from a concentration camp to a prison. The people of St. Lucie County, who are paying for this, feel gypped that they can't get near the ballplayers.

"There's a few Mets who are real stinkers. Kevin McReynolds doesn't like to sign, but not because he's arrogant. He's just a shy guy and doesn't want to be bothered.

"Strawberry? Darryl can demand $15,000 for three hours, so he doesn't care much for it. But I tell you, Ft. Pierce, Florida, threw a thing for the Mets year before last, they escorted them in and out, and when it was over the players ran to the bus to get away from the fans. The only player who stopped and signed was Strawberry. I guess you gotta get these guys on the right day."

Hotels: The team hotel is the Radisson Hotel, 10120 South Federal Highway, Port St. Lucie, FL 34952; (407) 337-2200. There is no hotel near the ballpark, but the St. Lucie West prospectus says, "Several motel sites are available to qualified operators with a sound financial background." (Translation: "If you want a room, *build* one.")

For something a little more substantial, try the Club Med Village Hotel Sandpiper (3500 Morningside Blvd., Port St. Lucie; (800) CLUB-MED). For over a thousand dollars a week per person, the Club Med takes care of everything—room, meals, golf, tennis, boating, wine. Over a thousand acres, two-and-a-half golf courses . . . well, you get the idea. A less costly alternative is the Holiday Inn Oceanside in Jensen Beach.

Area Attractions

- **Atlantic Ocean.** From St. Lucie West, head due east until further travel is prevented by water. Open round-the-clock, 365 days a year.
- **Bird-watching in the piney woods, St. Lucie West.** Walk 100 yards in any direction from the baseball complex boundaries and stop. Stand very still. Don't make noise. On a good day, you can expect to see white-eyed vireos, pine warblers, mockingbirds, and rufous-sided towhees. On a bad day, when bulldozers are ripping out the trees, keep an eye out for relocating screech owls and red-shouldered hawks.
- **Fruit.** The Indian River country produces the best citrus fruit in the United States. The oranges are irregularly shaped and sized, bruise easily, and are rarely uniform in color (not having been spray-painted), but that's how you know they're good. Various grove shops and roadside stands sell and box fruit for shipment back home.
- **Ft. Pierce Jai-Alai** on Kings Highway, one mile north of Exit 56 on the Florida Turnpike. For schedule, call (407) 464-7500. General admission is $1.

"A number of years ago, a young sportswriter was sent to Florida to cover the Mets. He was so eager, like the players, to do well, and he wrote with all his heart.

"In one of his first dispatches back to his paper in New York, he described how the hitters were hitting and the pitchers pitching and how the warm sun that morning had risen in the west.

"He quickly received a cable from his office. It read: 'Forget the Mets. Cover irregularity of the sun.' "

—Ira Berkow

FLORIDA HIGHWAYS: A PRIMER

The two-mile stretch of Prima Vista Boulevard leading to St. Lucie County Stadium will probably be choked with cars when you get there, but it's a drag strip in the morning when the players report to camp. The Mets had to hold a clubhouse meeting/traffic-safety school one spring because players kept getting tickets for doing sixty miles per hour in a forty-miles-per-hour zone.

You'll be lucky to do ten.

Florida, quite frankly, suffers from vehicular arteriosclerosis, and the quicker you learn how to avoid traffic jams, the better. Here are a few tips:

- Avoid the coast highways. On a map, U.S. 1 looks like the shortest route between Vero Beach and Port St. Lucie, but the map doesn't show the 400 traffic lights, mall entrances, lumbering vegetable trucks, and "35 mph" signs on the way. You're better off driving inland several miles and taking I-95. Same thing on the Shell Coast: Ft. Myers to Sarasota takes an eternity on U.S. 41, but it's a quick shot on I-75. Above St. Petersburg, it's a toss-up between Alternate 19—the coast road—and U.S. 19 or U.S. 41. They're all slow. (On the other hand, take A1A between any two points on the east coast if you're playing tourist. You'll average about twenty-five miles per hour, but the highway is often right on the ocean and the scenery is great.)
- Dare to stray from Interstate 4. Paradoxically, you are often better off taking state or county roads between towns in central Florida. Getting from Winter Haven to Lakeland via I-4 calls for miles of unnecessary driving. Just take one of the three-digit highways straight across to Lakeland and Plant City. They're good roads and lightly traveled
- Use the Florida Turnpike. It's expensive and deadly dull, but it's fast and safe (during baseball season, anyway—Jose Canseco isn't home).
- Shun Tampa. The rush hours are unbelievable there, even on the interstates, and they don't call the Frankland Bridge "The Car-Strangled Spanner" for nothing. Should you leave Dunedin or Clearwater as early as 2:30 P.M., you can count on it taking at least an hour to escape the outbound commuter traffic.
- Go to the beaches on a rainy day. Most of Florida's sandy spots are on barrier islands that can be reached only by bridge. Either there aren't enough bridges or the bridges aren't wide enough. Whatever the reason, the beach traffic can be hellacious.
- Approach Ft. Lauderdale and Miami with limited expectations and a cool head. I-95 is undergoing some minor touching-up that is expected to take thirty to forty years, so delays are possible.

On a serious note, please drive cautiously in the rain. Florida's highways, even the new ones, accumulate water in channels from traffic wear. Hydroplaning is a constant danger.

Mets

• **Deep-sea fishing and charter boats** embark from various marinas in Stuart and Jupiter. Stuart bills itself as the "Sailfish Capital of the World." Contact: The Stuart Sailfish Club, P.O. Box 2005, Stuart, FL 33495; (407) 286-9373.

Restaurants, Lounges, and Dives: "The players usually hang out at a place on the beach called Shuckers Two," says Tom Verducci, who covers the Mets for *Newsday.* "It's a sports-bar, game-room, Bennigan's-type place. Wednesday night is 'bikini-judging night,' and players tend to show up then. The place I would go is an Italian place called Casa Stefano on U.S. 1 in Stuart. Anything on that menu is good. If there's something you'd like that's not on the menu, they'll fix it for you. It's outstanding." John Harper of the *New York Post* agrees about Casa Stefano—"It's probably the best place we go"—and also recommends Mr. Laff's Riverfront in Jensen Beach: "It's a nice place on the water with a big bar. Two years ago the food was bad, but somebody bought it and redid it, and the food was great this year. There's also a place in Stuart, the Jupiter Crab House."

Dan Castellano of the *Newark Star-Ledger* gets the other writers' nod as the scribe with the best nose for restaurants, and he favors Casa Stefano ("I got it from Frank Cashen, he goes there all the time") and the Prawn Broker in Stuart.

"The worst thing about the Mets moving," moans Marty Noble of *Newsday* "is that they didn't bring Bern's with them from Tampa."

Chamber of Commerce: 1626 S.E. Port St. Lucie Blvd., Port St. Lucie, FL 34952; (407) 335-4422.

Spring Training Sites: 1962–87, St. Petersburg, FL; 1987–present, Port St. Lucie.

Won–Lost Record/Attendance:

Year	Record	Attendance
1989	12–18	94,490
1988	19–10	86,661
1987	12–14–1	61,534
1986	13–13–1	68,051
1985	13–12	38,731

Z.SMITH
34
SUTTER
42

STADIUM INFORMATION

Municipal Stadium
715 Hank Aaron Drive
West Palm Beach, FL 33401
(407) 684-6801 (Expos)
(407) 683-6100 (Braves)

How long at present location: Twenty-eight years (Braves) and ten years (Expos)
Capacity: 5,000
Dimensions: 330 feet down lines, 400 feet to center
Directions: From I-95, take Palm Beach Lakes Blvd. (Exit 53) east two blocks. Ballpark is on the right, next to the inverted cone of the "Leaky Teepee" (Municipal Auditorium).
Parking: Paved, plentiful, and free.

There are two ways to make a ballpark beautiful. The first is to build it that way in the first place. The second is to take what you have, however banal, and decorate it.

That's what they've done in West Palm Beach. Municipal Stadium, with its gray concrete and white fanfold roof, is a toddler's version of those modern big-city ballparks that baseball writer Tom Boswell once described as "mutant oil filters," but West Palm's decorator has done wonders with the place. The parking lot and perimeter areas are landscaped. A delightful alcove with picnic tables invites fans to picnic on the concourse behind home plate. Huge banyan trees, with their Tarzan-vine roots and vast canopies of shade, invite spelunkers into their cave-like recesses.

Then, to remind us that this is a baseball park and not an arboretum, a sign painter has been hired. Not a graphic-arts consultant, mind you, but an old-fashioned, honest-to-baseball, do-it-by-hand sign painter. (See sidebar.) Everywhere you turn, patiently waiting to serve you, is a sign—screwed to a door, wired to a fence, painted on a wall, perched on a pole: BASEBALL TODAY AT 1:05 . . . NO TRYOUTS DURING SPRING TRAINING . . . ENTRANCE TO CLUBHOUSE. None of that spray-paint-and-stencils stuff, either. These are graceful, nostalgic signs that celebrate old scripts and fonts the way old baseball cards celebrate baseball.

Finally—and for this we must give the architect his due—Municipal Stadium has one of spring baseball's best views. From the top of the shady grandstand, the daydreaming fan can pick up the far-off shapes of the Flagler Museum and the old Biltmore Hotel in Palm Beach, the gentle arcs of the bridges over the Intracoastal Waterway, and the pompous thrust of Donald Trump's new office tower at Phipp's Point. When a breeze is working, this high perch is the penthouse of Florida baseball.

Best of all, with two teams in residence, there is baseball every day.

Ticket Information: At press time, the Braves had not yet released their 1991 ticket prices. Last year's prices were box $8; grandstand $7; general admission $5. For grandstand tickets, write Braves Tickets, Municipal Stadium, 715 Hank Aaron Drive, West Palm Beach, FL 33401. For current prices and information, call

(407) 683-6100. Expos: box $8; reserved $7; general admission $5. Tickets available at the box office or by calling (407) 689-9121. Or write Montreal Expos, P.O. Box 3566, West Palm Beach, FL 33402. Tickets also available through TicketMaster.

Autograph Opportunities: "If you're looking for a Brave or an Expo, the best time is 7:30 to 8 o'clock in the morning," says Scott Winslow, owner of World Baseball Cards in Lake Worth, Florida. "The players have to be in the clubhouse by nine, so the early birds come in for coffee before eight. The last ones in won't sign, though, not at a minute to nine. They're running.

"There's nobody on either team that an autograph collector would consider super-tough. Ozzie Virgil, when he was here, was a tough nut, but Tim Raines is really nice. On a scale of one to ten, I'd call West Palm Beach a seven."

Hotels: The Braves' hotel is the Palm Hotel, 630 Clearwater Park Road, West Palm Beach, FL 33401; (407) 833-1234. The Expos stay at the Holiday Inn, 4431 PGA Blvd. (at I-95), Palm Beach Gardens, FL 33410; (407) 622-2260.

Both places look shabby after you've visited Palm Beach's landmark Breakers Hotel (1 S. County Road), which is so loaded up with tapestries, gilt, crystal chandeliers, and Renaissance-style ceiling paintings that you expect to see a wigged Mozart playing harpsichord in the lobby bar. Unfortunately, only a ballplayer can afford the $250-to-$350-a-night room rates.

For more affordable beachfront digs, move up to Singer Island, which has a Hilton, a Best West-

82
66

ern, and many other hotel and condominium properties.

Area Attractions

• **The Breakers Hotel,** 1 S. County Road, Palm Beach (see above). If you were in Paris you'd visit Versailles, so don't pass up the Breakers just because you're staying at Motel 6. Check out the lobby, the Mediterranean Ballroom, and the Florentine and Circle Dining Rooms, and then ask the desk clerk for a rate card on the way out (good for a laugh when you show it to your neighbors back home). Note: Gentlemen are required to wear jackets and ties in the public rooms after 7 P.M.
• Polo at the **Palm Beach Polo and Country Club,** 13198 Forest Hill Blvd., Wellington, FL 33414. High-goal polo with the world's greatest polo stars (and sometimes Prince Charles). Champagne and hot dogs at the concession stands and at least one Gabor sister in attendance at all times. Sundays, in season. For times and teams, call (407) 793-1113.
• **Golf.** The area's public courses and golf resorts are too numerous to list, but the two courses at the PGA National Golf Club (1000 Avenue of the Champions, Palm Beach Gardens, FL 33418) have hosted many pro tournaments, and they're open to the public. Call (407) 627-1804 for tee times. A less expensive alternative is the **West Palm Beach Country Club** (7001 Parker Ave., West Palm Beach, FL 33405), another former PGA Tour site and one of the best public courses in the South. Its phone number is (407) 582-2019.
• Greyhound racing at the **Palm Beach Kennel Club**, Belvedere and Congress Roads, West Palm Beach.
• Jai-alai at the **Palm Beach Jai-Alai Fronton**, 1415 W. 45th St.
• Shopping on Palm Beach's **Worth Avenue**, one of the premier (and priciest) shopping streets of the world. Four long blocks of designer dress shops, boutiques, art galleries, jewelry stores, and specialty stores, with big names like Gucci and Saks dropped for anchors. If the prices seem too steep, pop into Thrift, Inc. (250 Worth Ave.) and grab a used feather boa or an antique wheelchair. All proceeds from this volunteer-staffed operation go to area causes and charities, including the American Legion Baseball Association Post #12.
• **Fishing.** Charter boats and drop-line fishing expeditions (half-day and full day) leave from various marinas in the Palm Beaches. Check the Yellow Pages for the nearest dock.

Restaurants, Lounges, and Dives: Manero's, a steakhouse, has long been a Braves hangout. "I eat just about all my meals there," says *Atlanta Journal* sports editor Furman Bisher. "There are classier and fancier places, but the food is great—good steaks, good pork chops, good seafood—and they've got the best martinis in the world. It *looks* like a restaurant, and that's important when you get to be my age."

Sandy Keenan, who covers Big East Basketball for *Newsday*, recommends Doherty's on Royal Palm Way in Palm Beach. ("The best crab soup in all of Florida.")

Other local favorites include John G's at the Lake Worth Casino and Pier (spectacular breakfasts and long lines, but worth the wait), Proctor's on U.S. 1 in West Palm Beach (all-you-can-eat fried fish), and Prime Time in Lantana (great, great hamburgers). For a late-night snack, *Palm Beach Life* magazine recommends Testa's in Palm Beach.

Chamber of Commerce: 401 N. Flagler Drive, West Palm Beach, FL 33401; (407) 833-3711.

Spring Training Sites: Braves: 1901, Norfolk, VA 1902–04, Thomasville, GA; 1905, Charleston, SC; 1906, Jacksonville; 1907, Thomasville, GA; 1908–12, Augusta, GA; 1913, Athens, GA;

expos
400

1914–15, Macon, GA; 1916–18, Miami; 1919–20, Columbus, GA; 1921, Galveston, TX; 1922–37, St. Petersburg; 1938–40, Bradenton, FL; 1941, San Antonio, TX; 1942, Sanford, FL; 1943–44, Wallingford, CT; 1945, Washington, D.C.; 1946–47, Ft. Lauderdale; 1948–61, Bradenton; 1962, Palmetto, FL; 1963–present, West Palm Beach. Expos: 1969–71, West Palm Beach; 1972–80, Daytona Beach, FL; 1981–present, West Palm Beach.

> "Every year, when I return from baseball spring training, people ask me what I saw that I liked. Every year I answer 'spring training.' "
>
> —Frederick C. Klein

Won–Lost Record/Attendance (Braves):

Year	Record	Attendance
1989	16–12–1	75,942
1988	8–21	71,696
1987	16–14	62,218
1986	18–11	58,194
1985	18–11	69,126

Won–Lost Record/Attendance (Expos):

Year	Record	Attendance
1989	12–14–1	79,643
1988	17–13	53,199
1987	11–16	54,969
1986	10–21	35,180
1985	12–18	37,175

The Brushmeister of West Palm Beach

The man behind most of the hand-painted signs at Municipal Stadium is "retired" sign-painter Paul Zeeb. His biggest project each year is the huge Braves schedule board that greets arriving fans, but many of his lesser works hang throughout the stadium. Zeeb and his wife, Lucille, share a deceptive bungalow in a nearby working-class neighborhood. The Zeeb abode is stunningly decorated with sidewalk inlays, exotic plants, glossy cedar panels and decoupage, and a backyard water-and-sculpture garden worthy of Disneyland.

Q: How long have you been painting signs?
A: I've been at it since 1944, when I first came to town. I was free and single then *(smiles at wife)* and I came here to escape the cold. I ran out of funds, and one day I met somebody in a bar who needed a helper. He was painting signs for Coca-Cola. I learned pretty quick, and two weeks later I went into business for myself. I painted outdoor signs for Coke for thirty years, and I guess 95 percent of my work was for them. But that particular type of advertising petered out. I did Kentucky Fried Chicken, Pepsi now and then, the South Florida Fair, a bunch of others. I've painted fleets of trucks. I worked for Mayflower Van Lines and Allied Van Lines. I once painted a rooster on the bottom of a swimming pool.

Q: How long have you been doing the Municipal Stadium signs?
A: Seven or eight years. The way that got started is, I did work off and on for Manero's restaurant, over by the ballpark, and somebody at Manero's mentioned my name to Pete Skorput, who's the stadium coordinator. I was already doing the advertising in five or six small ballparks. I must have done thousands of those back-wall ads.

Signpainter Paul Zeeb

But Pete hired me because of Manero's. It's mainly the schedule board now, but I still do all the hand-lettered signs at the park.

Q: Do you work alone?
A: That's right, I have no help. I'm getting too old to climb up there, so I talked them into letting me do the schedule board on four-by-eight-foot panels. It takes two-and-a-half panels to do the job.

Q: How do you get the words to come out centered?
A: You start in the middle and work both ways. It's second nature.

Q: For years, the schedule board had that big Braves logo of the laughing Brave. Did you paint that freehand?
A: No, you use a pounce pattern.

Q: A what?
A: A pounce pattern. You make a line drawing on paper. Then you go over the lines with what's called a "pounce wheel," which is a little roller with teeth. The pounce wheel makes little holes in the paper. Next, you put the pattern down where you want to paint and go over all the lines with what's called a "pounce bag," which is a little bag of colored dust. When you pull the pattern off, your drawing is transferred to the surface in dust. You paint from that. (*Author's note:* This is the same technique used by Michelangelo to paint the ceiling of the Sistine Chapel.)

Q: How do you decide what the Brave will look like?
A: The ballclub provides me with proof sheets with all the approved type styles and club logos, and I work from those. They're pretty fussy about how their name is written. The Braves want a lot of color and flash. I kind of miss the Brave they had, though. They eliminated that for reasons I didn't quite understand.

Q: Even your smallest signs show great care and individuality. Why haven't you succumbed to the temptation to turn them out on an assembly line?
A: A person's gotta take a little pride in his work. I don't want to put on any airs, but I'm a little like da Vinci. Nobody ever came to him and said, "Hey, Leo, we need a dozen more Mona Lisas."

Q: True, but his paintings weren't left out in the rain and sun, either. How long does an original Paul Zeeb last?
A: Some of them last three or four years. Others take more of a beating from the sun and last only a year. I just bring them back and redo them, and if a sign is too far gone, I retire it.

Q: Speaking of retirement . . .
A: I started to retire ten years ago, but I didn't really mean it. I developed a skin problem. I became an albino and could no longer stay out in the sun. But the Braves keep calling me back, and I guess I'll keep painting the signs as long as I can.

Q: If you're at a ballgame, do you find your eye wandering off the game and onto your work?
A: *(Laughing)* I don't go to ballgames, I watch 'em on TV.

STADIUM INFORMATION

Ft. Lauderdale Stadium
5301 N.W. 12th Ave.
Ft. Lauderdale, FL 33309
(305) 776-1921

How long at present location: Twenty-eight years
Capacity: 7,461
Dimensions: 335 feet to left; 325 feet to right; 401 feet to center
Directions: From I-95, take Commercial Blvd. West to Yankee Blvd. and turn right; go to 12th Ave. and turn left. Ballpark is on right.
Parking: Grass and gravel, $2.00.

"The Yankees are the pits of the autograph world," says autograph collector Scott Winslow of Lake Worth. "Guys that were good on other teams, they get traded to the Yankees and become complete jerks."

Winslow's sentiments are shared by most autograph hounds, who routinely describe the glamorous Yanks as "really rude . . . unpleasant . . . downright mean." Understandably, then, Ft. Lauderdale Stadium has responded with beefed-up security and fenced-in parking to keep the players and fans apart. Those fellows in pinstripes you see signing baseballs at the stadium rails are probably rookies who haven't yet learned to say, "Take a hike, kid."

Almost every collector concedes that being a Yankee is no picnic. "Sure, the Astros are great," says collector Tom Bunevich of Tampa, "but if they had as many fans as the Yankees, they'd get hard, too. It's the demand that makes the Yankees so tough." Adds Winslow: "New York City is the haven for autograph dealers. No matter who they sign for, the players are suspicious that that person is going to turn around and sell it."

Indeed, the problem may be New York, where the crush of street hustlers and fast talkers teaches ballplayers to be wary of cons, dodges, and strangers in general—even kids. Radio reporter John Matthews recalls an incident that took place in the lobby of Manhattan's Sheraton Centre Hotel in 1980. "I'd say the kid was ten or eleven years old," Matthews says. "He was wearing a Royals road uniform, the light blue kind, with number '5' on the back and 'BRETT' in capital letters." The kid had been waiting in the lobby for hours. It was a vigil. "You remember something like that—a kid in a Royals uniform in a New York hotel lobby."

Matthews was stepping into an elevator when he became aware of a background commotion, the sound a group makes when something commands its attention. "It was George Brett crossing the lobby. And this kid was following George, trying to get him to autograph a baseball, but George wouldn't sign the ball." Brett sped up to catch the elevator. The kid stayed behind at the edge of the lobby, looking forlorn. "Stunned," Matthews says.

The doors closed.

"I looked at George, and he's in that catatonic type of trance he goes into sometimes. He'd been real sullen the night before after going hitless and dropping a pop-up in Boston. But suddenly his face changed, he came out of the

NY

trance. His look said, 'I didn't mean to do that.' You could see his mind working: The kid put on the uniform, probably came in from Nassau County, waited all afternoon to get a ball signed . . . and obviously the kid will always remember that he got blown away by George Brett. George said, 'I've gotta go out there and have some fun. I'm just too hyper.'

"That night, he hit the first pitch from Rudy May for an upper-deck home run, starting his thirty-game hitting streak. It was that hitting streak, you'll remember, that took his average up over .400 in August and September and made him even more of a celebrity than he already was. And those two things have always stuck together in my memory—George starting the hitting streak and George not signing the baseball for the kid in the hotel lobby."

Matthews's anecdote may not prove anything—after all, Brett is not a Yankee—but many collectors seem eager to blame the Big Apple for the Yankees' bad manners. "It's funny," says Winslow, "but when Yankees get traded away, they become nice guys again."

That's good news.

Ticket Information: box $10; reserved grandstand $8; reserved bleachers $5. (Most boxes are renewed by longtime ticket-holders.) Write New York Yankees, Ft. Lauderdale Stadium, 5301 N.W. 12th Ave., Ft. Lauderdale, FL 33309, or call (305) 776-1921.

Autograph Opportunities: "Ft. Lauderdale is low on the totem pole," says Scott Winslow. "Most autograph collectors don't even bother to go." For those who do, the pregame action is off the front-row railings, particularly at the low chain-link fence in front of the right-field bleachers. Players also sign where they enter the field between the grandstand and the bleachers, although it requires a lot of reaching through rails and tossing of baseballs and pens from the higher rows.

Hotels: The team hotel is the Ft. Lauderdale Marriott–Cypress Creek, 6650 N. Andrews Ave., Ft. Lauderdale, FL 33309; (305) 771-0440. Marriott's two other local hotels are more fun. The Marriott Harbor Beach is an expensive beachfront resort a short walk from the Bahia Mar yacht basin, where the fictional tough guy Travis McGee docked his houseboat, *The Busted Flush.* The Ft. Lauderdale Marriott Hotel and Marina, right across the Intracoastal Waterway, is actually in a marina; sleek yachts dock right beside the beautiful pool. At the other end of the 17th Street Causeway, you'll find the round, seventeen-story tower of the landmark Pier 66, which also can accommodate yachts. All of these hotels are convenient to Port Everglades, where glitzy cruise ships embark for Caribbean ports.

Less expensive rooms can be had up and down "The Strip," Ft. Lauderdale's beachfront stretch of U.S. A1A, made famous by rampaging hordes of hormone-driven students. Two Sheratons, the Yankee Trader and the Yankee Clipper, share the higher-end of the A1A market with the Ft. Lauderdale Beach Hilton, but smaller properties a block or two off the beach offer real bargains. Ask your travel agent.

Area Attractions

- **Beaches.** Ft. Lauderdale's seven miles of sand are world famous, even if for the wrong reasons. If you don't like college students, consider driving north or south to Pompano Beach, Dania Beach, or Hallandale Beach. Be prepared for heavy afternoon traffic and delays on the drawbridges crossing the Intracoastal Waterway.
- **Paddlewheel cruises on the Intracoastal Waterway.** *The Jungle Queen* departs three times daily (including a four-hour dinner cruise) from the Bahia Mar Yacht Basin. For prices and reservations, call (305) 462-5596. *The Paddlewheel Queen's* dinner cruise offers dancing

under the stars. For reservations, call (305) 462-5596.

• **Swamp-buggy rides at Everglades Holiday Park** (U.S. 27 and Griffin Road). This forty-five-minute narrated airboat tour includes an alligator-wrestling show and a visit to an Indian village. Adults $11, children under twelve $5.50. Call (305) 434-8111.

• **Ocean World**, on the approach to the 17th Street Causeway, is a world-class aquarium with sharks and rays and dolphins getting along splendidly. Adults $8.95, children four to twelve $6.95. Open daily, 10:00 A.M. to 6:00 P.M., (305) 525-6611.

• **Fishing.** For pier fishing, try Dania, Lauderdale-by-the-Sea, Pompano Beach, or Hillsboro. For charter boats, contact the Bahia Mar Yacht Basin, (305) 525-7174.

• **Six Flags Atlantis** (2700 Sterling Road, Hollywood) is billed as the "world's largest water park" and houses a collection of water slides and a giant wave pool. Adults $12, children under eight $10. Open daily at 11 A.M.

• **Butterfly World** in Tradewinds Park, 3600 W. Sample Road. A walk through a lush tropical rain forest, surrounded by thousands of fluttering paint palettes. Includes an aviary, breeding laboratory, and collection of unusual insects. Adults $6, senior citizens $4, children under twelve $4, children under three free. Open daily. (305) 977-4400.

• **The International Swimming Hall of Fame** pays homage to the likes of Esther Williams and Johnny Weissmuller and also operates an Olympic-size public pool. It's located at 1 Hall of Fame Drive, Ft. Lauderdale, FL 33316, (305) 462-6536.

• **Parimutuel sports:** jai-alai at the Dania Jai-Alai Fronton, 301 East Dania Beach Blvd.; harness racing at Pompano Park, 1800 S.W. 3rd St. in Pompano Beach; dog racing at the Hollywood Greyhound Dog Track, 831 N. Federal Highway, Hallandale; and horse racing at Gulfstream Park, U.S. 1 in Hallandale. According to former Yankees media relations director Harvey Green, the players prefer the dogs and ponies. "Not that many go to jai-alai. You can't read the form."

Restaurants, Lounges, and Dives: There is no one Yankee hangout, but you often see players, *sans* pinstripes, at Gibby's, a steakhouse, and at Shooters, a great watering hole on the Intracoastal Waterway. (You can get to Shooters on Ft. Lauderdale's new Water Taxi, which carries up to twenty people at a time to docks and restaurants on the Intracoastal. To call the "cab," phone (305) 565-5507.)

"Roland's is a pretty good place, too," says beat writer Michael Kay of the *New York Daily News.* "It's sort of a classy type of restaurant/bar. You've got to dress well to go in and it's got valet parking. Shooters is more of a fun-type atmosphere. There's also a place that all the writers go to for lunch, the Char Hut, that's supposed to have the best hamburgers in the country. We brought one back for George Steinbrenner one day, but he complained that it was too cold."

Former Yankee manager and player Lou Piniella recommends Christine Lee's, a Chinese restaurant in Inverrary. "I love all the food there," he says, "but I usually get the Lobster Cantonese. I also like the Sea Watch restaurant over on the beach. There, I get the swordfish."

Broadcaster and former Yankee great Phil Rizzuto is emphatic about his favorite. "It's an Italian restaurant in Pompano called La Veranda. Yogi goes there, all the ballplayers go there because it's so good. Everything is cooked to order and comes in big bowls, not those skimpy things you get in restaurants now. They make great *pasta fagiola.*"

A New York writer who shall remain nameless slinks in with a tip for those who want something "a little off-color": "Some of the Yankees spend time at the Doll House, a strip joint.

WBJAA
Reds

> "Don't tell me about the world. Not today. It's springtime, and they're knocking baseballs around fields where the grass is damp and green in the morning and the kids are trying to hit the curve ball."
>
> —Pete Hamill

You can walk in any time of night and see players and writers there. It's more of a strip emporium, really; it's not that sleazy. There are three of these places in Ft. Lauderdale—Solid Gold, Pure Platinum, and the Doll House, all owned by the same guy. Pure Platinum was big this year because they installed showers; the players would go over there to watch girls take showers. Food? Yeah, they have food, but I'd be dammed if I'd eat it."

ABC's Dick Schaap recommends the view and the food at Hollywood's Top of the Home. "Great stone crab place, good hangout."

With the Orioles leaving Miami, Ft. Lauderdale becomes the baseball outpost closest to Miami's great hangouts. "I hope there's always a team in Miami," Schaap said a year ago, "because Joe's Stone Crab is wonderful." Joe's (227 Biscayne St., at the tip of South Beach) is certainly worth a detour. Another sorry-to-see-you-go place is the English Pub on Key Biscayne, where players once explored the mysteries of steak-and-kidney pie.

The more adventurous baseball folk will still find their way down to Miami's S.W. 8th St., better known as "Little Havana." The prices are low, the restaurants are colorful, and the food is an experience. (Writer Tom Boswell's favorite is a place called Versailles. You'll spot a lot of politicians when election time draws near.) Cuban restaurants don't really get going till about 9:00 P.M., so you'll have time to drop into a tapas bar for appetizers.

"Joe's Stone Crab is the biggie," says *Sports Illustrated*'s Tim Kurkjian, "but we also go to a great place on Miami Beach called the Bistro. I don't think it's French . . . it's got all kinds of food. There's also a place called the Baltimore Orioles Lounge, or something. It's right across from Bobby Maduro Stadium. They have three pictures on the wall—Babe Ruth, Lou Gehrig, and Fred Lynn. Believe me, nobody goes in there. It's one of the worst places in the world."

Chamber of Commerce: 208 Southeast 3rd Ave., Ft. Lauderdale, FL 33301; (305) 462-6000.

Spring Training Sites: 1903–04, Atlanta; 1905, Montgomery, AL; 1906, Birmingham, AL; 1907–08, Atlanta; 1909, Macon, GA; 1910–11, Athens, GA; 1912, Atlanta; 1913, Hamilton, Bermuda; 1914, Houston; 1915, Savannah, GA; 1916–18, Macon, GA; 1919–20, Jacksonville, FL; 1921, Shreveport, LA; 1922–24, New Orleans; 1925–42, St. Petersburg, FL; 1943, Asbury Park, NJ; 1944–45, Atlantic City; 1946–50, St. Petersburg, FL; 1951, Phoenix; 1952–61, St. Petersburg, FL; 1962–present, Ft. Lauderdale

Won-Lost Record/Attendance:

Year	Record	Attendance
1989	16–15	99,461
1988	22–10	104,884
1987	14–15	101,628
1986	17–11	100,021
1985	15–12–1	91,219

STADIUM INFORMATION

Twin Lakes Park (training facility)
6700 Clark Rd.
Sarasota, FL 34241
(813) 923-1996

How long at present location: Two years
Directions: (To training camp) From I-75, take Sarasota/Clark Rd. exit (Exit 37) east for a quarter mile. Facility is on right.

The Orioles had to cancel a game at Bobby Maduro Miami Stadium a couple of years ago when rain leaked onto the infield through holes in the tarp. "They're probably bullet holes," said pitcher Bob Milacki.

Gallows humor, sure. The way the players and writers used to describe Miami Stadium, you expected to see Don Johnson and Uzi-toting drug dealers trading fusillades on the switchback ramps. When someone referred to a hit, you didn't know if he was talking about the official scorer or a contract killing.

The jokes may not have been fair to that old Miami neighborhood of warehouses and *bodegas*, but certainly the ambiance left something to be desired. Three years ago, on reporting day, the Baltimores arrived at the stadium to the musical accompaniment of a bomb-squad truck speeding by and found a man spread-eagled on the pavement with two cops holding pistols to his head. Young ballplayers are impressionable, and they took these events to be a sign of neighborhood decay.

So when the Orioles signed a three-year contract to use the Royals' former minor-league complex in Sarasota for two weeks every spring, the Baltimore players checked into the new camp with wide eyes and open mouths, like the Dead End Kids on their first visit to a farm. They found, in the words of *Sports Illustrated* writer Tim Kurkjian, "a picture of serenity. No bombs, no police, no muggings, just a gentle warm breeze rustling the lush, green grass."

They also found—and this is why management made the move—a baseball complex with four practice fields, a football-style coaching tower, twenty-nine mounds, a clubhouse with room for four hundred lockers, a weight room, and a cafeteria. (In Miami, the players lined up at the two batting cages like tired motorists at a Stuckey's restroom, but Sarasota has five cages. Club officials say that the average Oriole took two thousand fewer swings than the average Met by opening day.) With Menckenesque disdain, *Evening Sun* columnist Bill Tanton pointed out that the Orioles, when they were champions, "got along fine with one-and-a-half fields. Now that they're terrible, they have to have five fields."

It didn't take a Delphic oracle to read the entrails of that bird: The Orioles said goodbye to Miami Stadium. And that's sad, because even in its run-down state it was a memorable ballpark, a great train depot of a place with sports murals in the concourses and a corrugated-metal roof over the seats. It was a Latin ballpark, and it was easy to half close one's eyes and see an infield composed of guys named Chico, Zoilo, Manny, and Jesus.

NO
PETS
BICYCLES
PERROS
BICICLETAS
EL FLEA MARKET
REDLOBSTER

No sense getting sentimental, though. The half field down the left-field line was a joke, the ground crew's equipment made a junkyard out of the sideline in right, and the sea of empty seats at most games was downright depressing.

On the other hand, it *was* a ballpark. This spring, the Orioles will be nomadic, wandering by camel from oasis to oasis looking for a good nine innings. They will play their home games on the Gulf Coast, mostly at McKechnie Field in Bradenton and Ed Smith Stadium in Sarasota.

Ticket Information: At press time, the Orioles had not yet released their 1991 ticket information.

Autograph Opportunities: Good. Last spring, the Orioles came over to the railings a lot just to thank the spectators for coming. "There's nobody really tough on the Orioles," says Scott Winslow, the Lake Worth card-shop owner. "The last semi-tough guy they had was Eddie Murray, and he went to the Dodgers. The Orioles have a lot of young players, and young players are easy. You can hand a guy three or four cards when he's a rookie, and he'll get a kick out of it. And you can even read his signature." Says Tampa's Tom Bunevich, "The Orioles are a pretty easy team. I would put Cal Ripken in the quality mode, he's very accommodating."

Hotels: The Harley Sandcastle, 1540 Ben Franklin Dr., Sarasota, FL 33577; (813) 388-2181. The beachfront hotels and condos are on Siesta Key, Lido Key, and Longboat Key. (The Colony Beach and Tennis Resort, the Diplomat Resort, and Beach Castle are all on Longboat Key.) On the mainland, the Hyatt Sarasota is the major hotel, but there are many, many motels along the Tamiami Trail (U.S. 41).

Area Attractions

- **Golf.** PGA Tour star Paul Azinger, a Sarasota native, recommends the Bobby Jones Golf Complex in Sarasota, where he honed his game as a youngster. (Note the street sign on the access road: Azinger Way.) Cubs scout Buck O'Neil is a regular on this public facility, which features two eighteen-hole layouts and a nine-hole executive course. For tee times, call (813) 955-8097.
- **Beaches.** There is a large public beach on Siesta Key, as well as a smaller spot of sand by a lagoon called Turtle Beach. If your taste in beaches tends more toward Boardwalk, try Bradenton Beach, which has more than its share of souvenir shops, dingy bars, and bikini-clad girls clutching beer cans as if their balance depends on it.

See also Chicago White Sox, page 118.

Restaurants, Lounges, and Dives: The Orioles' P.R. director, Rick Vaughn, recommends Summerhouse on Siesta Key. "That's my favorite. Outstanding seafood, probably the best place down there. But there's a great stone crab place on Longboat Key, too—Moore's Stone Crab Restaurant."

Richard Justice, who covers the Orioles for the *Washington Post,* also recommends Moore's. "Another favorite of mine is Abbey's Oyster Bar. They have everything—fish, chicken wings, cold beer. And there's this breakfast place not far from the ballpark that is fantastic—Millie's."

At the mention of Millie's, Ken Nigro's eyes light up. "It's fantastic, the absolute *crème de la crème,*" says the Orioles' director of special projects. "It might be the best in the country. It's not one of those trendy, crusty diner places. The people who go in are nice, the service is good, and the food! They've got this homemade coffee cake that is out of this world. It's a must." Nigro also likes Abbey's, and says, "As they say in Florida: when in doubt, go for the red snapper."

See also Chicago White Sox, pp. 117–18.

Chamber of Commerce: 1551 2nd St., Sarasota, FL 34236; (813) 955-8187.

Spring Training Sites: 1954, Yuma, AZ; 1955, Daytona, FL; 1956–58, Scottsdale, AZ; 1959–88, Miami, FL; 1989–1990, Sarasota/Miami, FL; 1991, Sarasota, FL.

Won-Lost Record/Attendance:

Year	Record	Attendance
1989	14–15	34,502
1988	9–19	86,644
1987	13–15	54,749
1986	14–15	50,592
1985	14–14	55,349

8

The Great Debate: Florida vs. Arizona

"Arizona is a much nicer place to watch baseball. It's a much nicer place to play baseball. Swatting bugs and sweating in the Florida humidity is no picnic for player or fan."—Editorial in the *Tempe* (Ariz.) *Daily News Tribune,* March 13, 1989.

Is it true? Does Florida lead Arizona in humidity and bugs?

According to National Weather Service records, the mean daily relative humidity at 5:00 P.M. for the month of March is 24 percent for Phoenix and 23 percent for Tucson. Relative afternoon humidities for the same month in Florida range from 50 to 60 percent in Orlando, 55 to 67 percent in Tampa, and 56 to 65 percent in Miami.

Arizona is definitely less sweaty.

On the bug front, the best authority is *Sports Illustrated*, which in a 1986 survey asked two questions of baseball's best minds: 1) Which are America's buggiest ballparks? and 2) What insect would you nominate, by city and species, for the Baseball Bug All-Star Team?

Only one current spring-training site was mentioned among the Top 10 Buggiest Ballparks—Lakeland-Plant City, FL, which placed third. However, *four* Florida insects made the nine-bug All-Star Team. They were:

- The Ft. Myers Mole Crickets. "The toughest bug I ever faced," according to famed groundskeeper George Toma. Mole crickets have stiff, digging forelegs and strong, thrusting hindlegs, enabling them to burrow like moles through compacted soil. In ballparks, they feed on turfgrass roots, and one determined mole cricket can churn up a hundred-yard furrow overnight. Says Toma, "I don't think there's a Roto-tiller on the market that could do a better job."
- The Dodgertown Fruit Flies. The Dodgers call them "blind mosquitoes," but they are neither blind nor mosquitoes. A swarm of these medium-sized flies swept through Holman Stadium a few springs back during an exhibition game, driving fans out of the stands and forcing players on the bench to drape towels over their heads.
- The West Palm Beach Fire Ants. Family *Formicidae*, subfamily *Myrmicinae.* Mean biters and voracious eaters, these ants have the unique ability to swarm on an animal or person and not bite until they have sufficient numbers to kill or maim. "A player might be standing on a fire ant mound and not know it for thirty seconds," says John Proctor, a research manager for the Mobay Chemical Corporation. "All of a sudden the ants say, 'It's time,' and they all bite at once."
- The Miami Termites. They were 1986's MVB—Most Valuable Bugs. A mature termite colony consumes only one-fifth of an ounce of wood a day, but these termites tried to make ballpark-bug history by actually eating Bobby Maduro Miami Stadium. "We have lots of termites," admitted former Orioles public relations director Bob Brown. "Wherever there's wood—the desk, the doorways—you'll usually find little wood piles."

No Arizona bug or ballpark merited mention in the *SI* poll, but two readers rose to the defense of Arizona bugs. One letter writer reported an infestation of flying ants that disrupted a softball tournament in Oracle, Arizona, north of Tucson, in 1978. "They were so thick, the pitcher appeared to be only a shadow, and everybody was flailing uncontrollably, trying to clear away the insects; of course, the game was stopped. Then suddenly all the ants died, and the entire area was covered with about an inch of dead bugs—home plate, automobiles, and everything in the snack bar. It remains to this day the most remarkable phenomenon I have ever seen."

Another reader remembered a mass of green leafhoppers that broke up a fast-pitch softball game in Gila Bend, Arizona. "The cloud was so thick that the outfielders couldn't see the ball, and batters were swinging at anything for fear of being hit by a pitch. Reports the next day indicated that the cloud of bugs reached three miles high and five miles wide and eventually covered a distance of twenty miles."

Neither of these outbreaks, however, took place during a spring-training game.

Twins

STADIUM INFORMATION

Lee County Sports Complex
1410 Six Mile Cypress Parkway
Ft. Myers, FL 33912
(813) 335-2284 (for information)

How long at present location: First year
Capacity: 7,500
Dimensions: 330 feet down lines, 380-foot alleys, 405 feet to center
Directions: Take I-75 to Exit 21 (Daniels Rd.), go west to Six Mile Cypress Parkway. Turn south, go one and a quarter miles.
Parking: Room for 2,829 cars. Fee to be announced.

"This club isn't owned by baseball people anymore," a Twins executive said two springs ago. "It's owned by businessmen. And they're experts in brinksmanship."

He was talking about negotiations with local government to keep the Twins in Orlando, where they have trained for all but three of the last fifty-four years, counting their previous incarnation as the Washington Senators. The Twins wanted between $4.5 and $5.5 million spent on upgrading Tinker Field—a grandstand extension, new locker rooms, etc.—but the local politicians offered somewhat less. Result: the Twins open this spring in a squeaky-new complex in Ft. Myers.

Ft. Myers, of course, is the town that said no when the Kansas City Royals asked for similar improvements to Terry Park in 1987, causing the Royals to jump to *their* sparkling new complex at Boarded-up and Baseball. That's how the game is played these days, and any team reluctant to keep its mistress happy with bracelets and bonbons can be sure the sweet young thing will run off with another town.

There's not much point in dwelling on Tinker's charms (starting with the fact that it was named for Joe Tinker, the shortstop of Tinker-to-Evers-to-Chance fame), because Tinker is history. Instead, the Twins and their fans should concentrate on what they have to look forward to in Ft. Myers: good restaurants, beautiful beaches, warm days, ungodly traffic, affordable golf, condos on the water . . . and the Screecher. (The Screecher is an eccentric senior citizen who haunted Royals games for years, walking through the stands going, "Whoooop! . . . Whoooop! . . . Whoooop!" in a loud and unforgettable falsetto.)

Kansas City Royals coach John Mayberry says he, for one, will be glad to see Ft. Myers back in the Grapefruit League, if only to visit a restaurant called the Wagon Wheel. "Ham hocks," he recalls with a dreamy smile, "cabbage and rice, pinto beans, hot water corn bread, peach cobbler. Hmmmm-*hmmmm.* Those soul sisters can cook!"

Good times ahead for Mayberry's palate, but the Twins move is sure to taste sour to those left behind in Orlando.

Ticket Information: box $8; reserved $6; pavilion (upper four rows of grandstand) $4. At press time, the Twins planned to limit season ticket sales to 4,000. Individual game sales begin December 3, and there's a $3 service

charge for mail orders. For spring training ticket information, write to Minnestoa Twins Season Tickets, 501 Chicago Ave. So., Minneapolis, MN 55415, or call (612) 375-7454. Walk-up sales begin January 14.

Autograph Opportunities: "The Twins have got some toughies," says Tampa card-shop owner Tom Bunevich. "Kirby Puckett's pretty cooperative, although he's a bit of a scribbler. But Kent Hrbek's still a jerk. Always has been."

Hotels: The Twins had not yet selected their team hotel at press time. The Ft. Myers Sheraton is the biggest and slickest hotel in town, but the author can't recommend it (explanation below). The Royals used to stay at the Ramada Inn (2220 W. 1st St.)—thin walls, plastic glasses, and hot and cold running bugs, but a pleasant pool area and a great location on the Caloosahatchee River. Ditto for the Riverfront Inn next door, except the pool is second-rate. The Robert E. Lee Motor Inn is a good choice if you don't mind being on the opposite bank; good river views from many of the rooms. Golfers and tennis players will enjoy the Cape Coral Inn and Country Club (4003 Palm Tree Blvd., Cape Coral), which offers golf packages and rooms with fairway views. There are also numerous motels on Cleveland Ave. (Highway 41), as well as a new Marriott Courtyard just off Colonial Boulevard.

Most of the players and writers rent condos on the beach. The best bargains are near Ft. Myers Beach, but the beauty spots are on Sanibel Island. Both areas require bridge crossings and long commutes in heavy beach traffic, but it's worth the trouble.

Author's Revenge Department

In their last year at Ft. Myers, the Royals stayed at the Sheraton, across the street from the downtown marina. When a cold snap hit, my wife and I had to call the front desk to complain that our room was uninhabitable. We weren't cold, we were *hot*—the room air conditioner kept going off.

The unsympathetic night manager insisted that nothing was wrong. "The air conditioners are designed to go off when the outside temperature is below sixty-five," he said. "It's an energy conservation measure."

"I'm not interested in the outside temperature," I said. "I'm interested in the *inside* temperature. It must be ninety in our room, and the windows don't open."

"Sir, the air conditioners are designed . . ."

This went on for half an hour, and I couldn't convince the fellow that air conditioners are designed to cool rooms. He refused to send up a maintenance man or move us to another room, and my wife and I spent the early morning hours pacing the lobby—which, curiously enough, was cool.

The next day, I threw a tantrum sufficient to get the day manager to send up the hotel "engineer." This fellow, at least, was rational. He confided that guests had been screaming for weeks, and the reason we couldn't change rooms was because all of the rooms were the same. He opened up the air conditioner and pulled out a metal wand connected to a cable. "This is the thermostat," he said. "If the air conditioner stops, grip this tightly in your hands for a couple of minutes to warm it up. Better yet, get a warm cat to sleep on it."

Sure enough, the air conditioner ran for about three minutes after he warmed up the wand. Then it clunked off.

Terrific! All we had to do to stay cool was get up every five minutes and sit on the floor in the dark clutching the thermostat.

I could go on to describe several more clashes with the hotel staff over this matter, but suffice it to say that they were unfailingly unhelpful and implied that we were out of line for complaining. When we checked out after three sleepless nights, we got no apologies and no adjustment on our room bill.

I wouldn't stay at this hotel again on a dare.

Area Attractions

• **Beaches.** For pelicans, pier fishing, beer guzzling, and souvenir shops, your best bet is Ft. Myers Beach, fifteen miles south of Ft. Myers. If you prefer nature in its unspoiled state, your better options are Sanibel and Captiva Islands, where the seashell-hunting is world famous and dolphins come into waist-deep waters to frolic. To get there, take McGregor Blvd. (Highway 867) west and have several dollars ready for the toll bridge. Sanibel has numerous restaurants and a few small shopping centers.

• **Golf.** Among the numerous resort and public courses in the area, Lochmoor Country Club is probably the best golf for the price. Lochmoor has twilight rates for the baseball fan who likes to play after the ball game, and they even let afternoon golfers carry their bags instead of renting carts. Good practice range, too. For tee times, call (813) 995-0501.

• **The Thomas Alva Edison house,** 2350 McGregor Blvd., was the inventor's winter home and laboratory for more than forty years. Today it is a museum and botanical garden, and there are few home tours in the country to match it. Open daily. Adults $5; children six to twelve $1; children under six free. Call (813) 334-3614 for further information.

Restaurants, Lounges, and Dives: "There's this place downtown in an old Victorian home," recalls *Kansas City Star* sportswriter and author Jack Etkin. "A very interesting place with lots of period rooms and excellent food." That place is called the Veranda, and it's actually an antebellum mansion devoted to Southern-style cooking. "It's *wonderful,*" gushes Nancy Hamilton of the Ft. Myers Visitor & Convention Bureau, but she declines to recommend a specific dish. "There's too many good things."

"Another great place is the Prawn Broker," says Etkin. "It's fairly far out on McGregor Boulevard, but it's worth the drive. I'm not a bottom-of-the-sea seafood lover, but I thoroughly enjoyed the grouper, and I never even tried grouper before I went to Florida."

Other favorite restaurants from the Royals era include Smitty's, an excellent steak and salad-bar place next to the Ramada Inn; the Chart House seafood restaurant on 1st Street; and, of course, the author's choice—Morrison's Cafeteria, now with two Ft. Myers locations.

Chamber of Commerce: 1420 Jackson St., Ft. Myers, FL 33902; (813) 332-3624. Also, the Lee County Visitor and Convention Bureau, 2180 W. 1st St., Suite 100 (PO Box 2445), Ft. Myers, FL 33902-2445; (800) 237-6444.

Spring Training Sites: (As Washington Senators) 1901, Phebus, VA; 1902–04, Washington, D.C.; 1905, Hampton, VA; 1906, Charlottesville, VA; 1907–09, Galveston, TX; 1910, Norfolk, VA; 1911, Atlanta, GA; 1912–16, Charlottesville, VA; 1917, Atlanta, GA; 1918–19, Augusta, GA; 1920–29, Tampa, FL; 1930–35, Biloxi, MS; 1936–42, Orlando, FL; 1943–45, College Park, MD; 1946–1990 (as Twins since 1961), Orlando; 1991, Ft. Myers.

Won–Lost Record/Attendance:

Year	Record	Attendance
1989	19–12	58,796
1988	11–18	51,094
1987	14–10	52,268
1986	11–9	58,505
1985	13–16–1	48,451

Baseball Card Photographer Michael Ponzini

Never mind the dew on the outfield grass. Never mind the sun climbing over the hulking silhouette of the Citrus Bowl. This looks like the booking desk at the county jail. A ballplayer, ill at ease, stands near the first-base dugout and stares woodenly at the empty seats while a bearded man in a multipocketed hunting vest takes his mug shot. *(Flash . . . Flash . . .)* The ballplayer turns around, showing his back, and the bearded man takes another picture. *(Flash).*

The bearded man is Michael Ponzini, a free-lance photographer from New York. He does not work for the police. He is on assignment for Topps, the baseball card company.

Q: Why the back shots?
A: I know the veterans' faces pretty well, but the young guys, I make sure I shoot their number. You'd hate to have a guy's first card come out with the wrong player on it.

Q: You work fast.
A: When you're shooting an entire club, you don't have time to get too creative with a pose. Forty-five seconds to a minute, that's all I have. I do a whole team in two or three days.

Q: Are the players cooperative?
A: Most of the younger guys get a kick out of posing for a baseball card, but the veterans don't care that much. Certain players—I won't mention names—really dislike posing. They would prefer an action photo for their card. Charley Kerfeld of the Astros, he was funny last year. He wanted one of those old-fashioned poses from the fifties, where the pitcher has released the ball and he's bent over with his glove

Sports photographer Michael Ponzini

open waiting for the ball to be hit back to him. He was adamant about it, "Be sure you use this pose." It was fairly legitimate, but hokey-looking.

Q: Have any players tried to fool you by wearing a glove on the wrong hand or something like that?
A: They've tried, but you try to remember which way they bat or throw. Sometimes a pitcher will fool around and try to pose with a bat, just to get a goof card in there.

Q: The Bill Ripken card, the one with the obscenity on the bat handle. Was that a goof card?
A: That was Fleers, so I couldn't say. I know Topps is very careful not to let something like the obscenity on the Ripken card get through. They don't want to embarrass themselves or the player. Even the goof shots with the guys posing the wrong way, they don't even want that. They want the card right.

Q: Does anybody flat-out refuse?
A: Occasionally. If a player won't pose, that's his prerogative. Someone in the Topps office will handle it.

Q: What's the most common player complaint?
A: Stale poses. Actually, the players are becoming more conscious of what goes on their card. You get more suggestions.

Q: What happens if the player blinks at the wrong moment or looks uncommonly stupid when you print the picture?
A: We'll do it over. Topps doesn't like to depict a player in a poor fashion. We want the players to be happy with their cards. We want them to look at them with affection years from now.

Q: What's the favorite card you've shot?
A: One that stands out in my mind is an action shot of Tony Perez in his last season with the Reds. He had just hit a home run, and he was crossing home plate and exchanging a high-five with Eric Davis, who had his back to me. Perez had a really nice expression on his face.

Q: Do all the players get action shots as well as posed shots?
A: We try. We do the poses so we're covered if we can't get the player in action. But we try to shoot various things for each player, so Topps can choose. There's a lot of luck involved. You can shoot very heavy on a player during a game, and you might still end up with nothing but a standard batting stance. If he's swinging well, you might get a good follow-through shot. Outfielders are pretty tough because you need a real large lens to capture action in the outfield, and a lot of times there *isn't* any action in the outfield. Catchers are a little easier. They get the ball every pitch.

Q: How hard is it to get a really good action shot? Baseball is somewhat unpredictable.
A: A lot of it is anticipation and a lot of it is luck. You'll anticipate the play at the plate, shoot it, and sometimes it turns out great and sometimes it turns out blah. Or you might anticipate the play, but not get the focus needle-sharp. You edit the film later and you want to cry, but all you can do is try again the next day.

Q: And shoot a lot of film.
A: Oh, yeah. On an average game, I'll shoot about twenty rolls of film, thirty-six exposures per roll.

Q: Did you collect baseball cards when you were a kid?
A: Oh, sure—I had the shoeboxes. I guess baseball cards were the first thing that interested me in photography. When I was still pretty green, I approached Topps about shooting for them, and they let me shoot a few games. That was in '82. Their Number-One photographer, Mickey Palmer, took me under his wing and taught me. He's kind of a giant in the field of photography, and I was very fortunate to learn under him.

Q: Is it fun work?
A: On a good day, it's great. On a bad day *(grinning)* it's a lot of frazzled nerves.

Quoting from Scripture

It'll be midnight in the hotel bar when they start telling Billy Scripture stories. One baseball man will put down his margarita and say, "Remember when ol' Billy Scripture stormed out of the dugout with a gun and shot that seven-foot rattlesnake on the mound in Sarasota?"

"Yeah, and he turned up the next day wearing a snakeskin belt and hatband!"

Another will say, "Did you hear about the time in Columbus when Billy climbed the tower in right field and did chin-ups from the light rack?"

The laughter will bring the waitress over to find out what's so funny, and a baseball man will say, "Sweetheart, we're talking about a fellow who was so tough he used to bite the covers off baseballs. He was so strong you could put six 200-pound ballplayers on a table and he'd lift the whole load on his back."

"I've heard of him," she'll say. "Paul Bunyan, right?"

And that'll prompt them to tell the original Billy Scripture story: How when he was an all-America outfielder at Wake Forest University, he heard that cutting wood was the best exercise for a hitter, so he went out into the North Carolina woods and felled giant white oak trees by moonlight. *Chunk . . . chunk . . . chunk . . . .*

"You talk about hot water! By the time they caught him, Billy had cut down half the hardwoods in the campus preserve."

"He couldn't pay for the damage, so as punishment they made him cut the trees into firewood for the faculty. He about got expelled!"

Billy Scripture: baseball manager, woodchopper, world-class trapshooter, hunting guide, champion cusser. Spent nine years as a player in the Orioles and Mets organizations; became a minor-league manager for the Royals, got fired; joined the Pirates organization, didn't like the contract they offered and disappeared. "Think he's got a gun shop in Virginia Beach," says a writer covering the International League. "Last I heard, he was managing someplace in New Hampshire," says an ex-player, "but he may be out of baseball now."

And still the stories. How Scripture would straddle home plate and let a pitching machine bounce fastballs off his chest. How he would have several players hold one end of a fungo bat while he twisted the other end till the bat splintered.

A major-league general manager says, "I once saw him bite a piece out of the bench, just to show how strong he was."

A big-league trainer says: "You know how they bundle up newspapers with heavy-gauge wire? Billy would pick up a stack and bite the wire off."

Scripture, you might decide, is a myth. Indeed, *The Baseball Encyclopedia*, which lists all the players who ever played major-league ball, has no entry for him. You won't find his name in an Orioles, Mets, Royals, or Pirates media guide. Directory assistance in Virginia Beach, Virginia, never heard of him. ("I show an *Earl* Scripture. Could that be your party?")

You have to dig. There is a tiny "Scorecard" item in the July 7, 1975, *Sports Illustrated* about the manager of a last-place Southern League team who took out his frustration by chewing the covers off baseballs. ("Only lost one molar so far, and that's a whole lot less expensive than an ulcer operation.")

If you don't mind dust, there are old organization books in a back room at Royals Stadium in Kansas City. They show that an Earl Wayne Scripture, Jr. ("nickname—Bill") was once the Royals minor-league coordinator of instruction; that he was a five-foot nine-inch, 200-pound man of Scottish-English descent, born in Pensacola, Florida, who trained Labrador retrievers as a hobby; that he played a summer of semipro ball for the Alaska Goldpanners of Fairbanks;

and that in 1967 he led the Eastern League in times hit by pitched balls.

And somewhere in the vaults of the National Broadcasting Company there is probably still a videotape of a flaky coach showing baseball announcer Joe Garagiola how to bunt holding the bat vertically instead of horizontally. ("Hey, the ball can't hit your face. The bat's in the way.")

But those who knew him don't have to dig for memories of Scripture. "He's about on the edge of folklore," says Royals trainer Mickey Cobb. "The first time I saw him, I was visually stunned by the way he was built. He looked like he was etched out of stone. Massive jaw structure, flat stomach, thick hands, a shaved head. He was very fastidious. His uniform had a crease in it, and his helmet had to be just so.

"He was tough, maybe the toughest I've ever seen. I remember a time when he had nineteen blisters on one hand from hitting. He just came in and poured alcohol on it. No Band-Aids. Other times, he would deliberately have someone hit flies out to the warning track so he could practice running full speed into the chain-link fence."

A crazy man? A sociopath? "Naw," Cobb says. "Personally, I found him to be a great joy."

"He wasn't a giant," recalls Pirates player development director Buzzy Keller, "but you talk about wound tight. I've seen him take a fungo bat and break it on his chest."

A show-off? A hot dog? Keller shakes his head. "He wasn't a kook by any stretch of the imagination. He was a very, very dedicated instructor."

"The most consistent thing about him," counters Royals general manager John Schuerholz, "is that he got fired all the time. His priorities in life were: one, shooting skeet; two, dogs; and then baseball. He's not so remarkable—just bizarre." Schuerholz shrugs. "He *was* a good baseball man, I'll give him that."

Branch B. Rickey, former minor-league director for the Pirates, says of Scripture: "There were people who would complain that he was tough to work with, but there was never any question about his competence as an instructor or manager. Almost everybody remembers him fondly. It's just that Bill's singularness of purpose sometimes clashed with the aims of individual minor-league franchises. With Bill, there was not a lot of accommodation to the owner's needs."

Actually, the most consistent thing about Billy Scripture is this: Baseball people talk about him as if he were dead.

* * *

But he's not. Here he is now, in fact, working in a closet-size room in the steel and cinder-block shellhouse at the Orange County Trap and Skeet Club in Orlando. Black cowboy hat, blue jeans, boots, a polo shirt stretched over massive shoulders and a no-longer-flat stomach. A twenty-diamond gold bracelet engraved with his nickname, "Billy."

It is four in the afternoon, and the forty-five-year-old Scripture has been at it since before dawn, twelve hours straight, and he will continue until near midnight, keeping targets flying for prosperous snowbirds competing in a week-long trapshooting tournament, Orlando's link in the Florida Chain Shoot. Neither the muffled blasts of nearby shotguns nor the news that he is 400 boxes short of targets for the weekend shakes his calm. Unlike the old days, Scripture is not about to eat a baseball or climb a light tower.

"Hey, I'm sane and sober now," he says, striking a match to light a thin cigar. The tiny phosphorous flare illuminates the labels of cans on a shelf by his head: BALL POWDER . . . SMOKELESS POWDER . . . FLAMMABLE. He shakes out the match. "Someone's always runnin' in here sayin' there's a problem." He blows a cloud of smoke. "There's no problem. I haven't any idea where I'm gonna get 400 boxes of targets, but I'll get 'em. I'll get 'em if I have to effing *invent* 'em."

There's nothing in Scripture's manner to suggest that he has been exiled, though you might expect it from a man who has been living in a hotel since May, 1986, when he took over management of the gun club. "I didn't get tired of baseball," he says. "I wasn't burned out. I just wanted to shoot full time." He nods toward the storeroom door, on which is written: THERE IS NO SECOND PLACE . . . EVER. "You have to have a hell of a lot of determination to win in this game, just like baseball. You line up toe-to-toe and put your money on the line."

Plus, there's something to be said for a life free from organizational inertia and red tape. "Sometimes I thought baseball was just an effing game of perpetual ignorance. You could come up with a better way to do something and they still wouldn't change their minds. 'Cause that's the way it had always been done. Baseball is full of people who manage scared, play scared, and *lose* scared."

He pushes his hat back on his head. "I probably couldn't manage in baseball today, because I'm probably the most hard-nosed S.O.B. in the world. A lot of managers are basically excuse-makers. That is an effing weakness. A character flaw. I love shooting, because it is a no-excuse environment. You either hit that sucker or you don't."

The door opens and Glenda Scripture, Earl's wife, steps in. She is down for the week from their home in Virginia Beach to serve as a tournament cashier, taking entry fees and paying out cash prizes to the daily winners. Behind her is a red-faced, beefy shooter with a complaint about a scorekeeper/puller. In the nearby clubhouse, cardplayers laugh raucously.

Scripture calmly takes care of business and then heads for his red pickup truck. "You think the damned baseball players are crazy," he says with a grin, "you oughta see some of these people!"

Another shooter, who has just come from the scoreboard, watches with admiration as Scripture hops into the truck. Scripture is the winner of that afternoon's fifty pairs doubles, an event in which the shooter fires at pairs of targets released simultaneously in different directions. His scores: 99 out of 100. "Earl put the hurt on 'em, didn't he? Ninety-nine, that's damn good shooting."

The next afternoon, Scripture competes in the daylong singles championship—200 targets at sixteen yards on eight different fields. The gun club's layout and ambiance are that of a golf driving range, except that these shooting sticks are made by Perazzi and Ljutic and cost $3,000 to $4,000 each. Expensive campers and RVs crowd the gravel lot behind the firing line.

"There's no poor people in this game," Scripture explains, cruising in a golf cart behind the shooters. "You have to have a lot of money and freedom to pursue it. Otherwise, you're just a local club shooter."

Scripture is no local club shooter. His Amateur Trapshooting Association classification is the highest, AA-27-AA. The double A's mean he averages at least 97x100 in singles competition and 93x100 in doubles; the 27 means he shoots from twenty-seven yards, the longest distance in handicap events. From 1981 to 1983, during a sabbatical from baseball, Scripture won four Virginia state championships—two singles and two all-arounds. He took the 1982 singles trophy with a perfect 200x200.

It's difficult to translate these scores into dollars. Unlike professional golfers, serious trapshooters put up their own money for tournament prizes in a complicated wagering system. There is no official earnings list, and it's anybody's guess who is making how much.

"I don't like to talk about the money," Scripture says. "You alarm some people and tick others off. I'll say this: The average shooter, if he takes a leave of absence from his job to try this full time, he'll be back in thirty days. Very few people can truthfully say they make a living shooting. There's a handful of men making very good money, maybe nine or ten."

Is Scripture one of them?

He pulls his hat down over his eyes. "I ain't sayin'."

He does not hesitate, however, when asked whether he was better at baseball or shooting. "*Much* better shooter. Baseball was hard for me. I had some good college years and all that, some All-America years that don't amount to a hill of beans. But I had very limited ability. I was proud I got as much out of my ability as I did." Shooting came easier to Scripture, who grew up on a South Carolina tobacco farm surrounded by woods and game. "My dad could shoot, and he taught me most of what I know."

Scripture parks the cart at Field Three for the next round of twenty-five targets. The firing is brisk, each man yelling "Pull!"—or in Scripture's case, grunting "Yeuhhmph!"—firing and reloading. Shooters change stations five times per round; the various stations, combined with the seventy-two angles in the "fan" of the trap launcher, simulate the unpredictability of real birds rising from the brush. Spent shells surround the shooters; target fragments litter the field.

Scripture misses three targets in this round. "I'm not shooting anywhere near my potential now," he says, returning to the cart. "It's the same as golf. If a guy wants to be a good tournament shooter, that's got to be his first priority."

Guiding the cart to another field, Scripture pulls up behind four burly adults and a curly-haired kid in jeans and T-shirt who is barely a hand taller than his shotgun. The boy is Scripture's thirteen-year-old son, Jason, vacationing from Virginia Beach so he can embarrass his elders. "I really believe Jason's gonna be an outstanding shooter," his father says. "He's already won a couple of major handicaps. Shot their asses off." He watches approvingly as his son shatters twenty-four out of twenty-five targets. "Of course, he doesn't know what pressure is yet, 'cause I'm paying for everything. He's just farting around."

As shooters gather around Scripture and exchange gun talk, it's plain his reputation as a teacher has followed him from baseball. "He can teach anything," says Cynthia Sutton, a young woman who has just come off the firing line. Scripture shrugs off the compliment. "Teaching is such a simple damn thing. I've never understood why people in baseball have so much trouble with that. You just slow it down, break down the mechanical motor skills, then you put it back together."

He learned that lesson first in the Orioles farm system, playing for managers like Cal Ripken, Sr., Joe Altobelli, Darrell Johnson, and Billy DeMars. The lesson was reinforced at the Royals' short-lived but innovative Baseball Academy in Sarasota. Scripture studied and taught baseball fundamentals there alongside the late Charlie Lau.

"I loved the Academy environment. Charlie and I sat and talked for days, watched tapes, broke everything down. That's what made him such a great batting coach." Scripture stops the cart. "Baseball would do well to make sure they have the best people at the rookie-league level. That first manager makes a hell of an impression on those kids."

It's Scripture's turn to shoot again, and this time he hits all twenty-five targets. After he returns to the cart, an obvious question arises: which is the easier target, a baseball or a clay pigeon?

"Well, I tell ya," he says, reaching for a cigar. "I can hit these, and I couldn't hit a curveball, so these must be easier."

* * *

Couldn't hit a curveball?

Although he played five seasons in Triple A, Billy Scripture never had the proverbial cup of coffee in the majors. "It was an effing struggle to play," he concedes. "The ball always fell a foot short." His lifetime average was .252.

His managerial record, measured in wins and losses, was similarly undistinguished. The sign on the door may say, "There is no second place . . . ever," but second place is the highest a Billy Scripture-led team ever finished.

"He was always into self-improvement techniques," says the Pirates' Rickey. "He jumped into psycho-cybernetics and then into visualization, and I can't remember what else." Rickey recalls a restaurant dinner with Scripture years ago. While they talked, Scripture's eyes remained fixed on a candle in the middle of the table. "He would perform eye exercises like that—following the tip of the flame, trying to hold his concentration while talking normally."

Scripture trained and toughened his body, too, with weights and old-fashioned calisthenics—thousands and thousands of push-ups, sit-ups, and knee bends. Like Watergate conspirator G. Gordon Liddy, who tested himself by holding his palm to a flame until the flesh was scorched, Scripture abused his body, saying, "If you're going to be a great athlete, you've got to withstand pain." He established a high standard of personal courage. Says the Royals' Cobb: "I never saw him duck away from a pitch. He would simply move his head out of the way as the pitch went by his nose." Others remember him killing the rattlesnake, not with a gun on the mound, but with a fungo bat at the warning track, or even with his bare hands by the locker room.

Scripture encouraged players to follow his example. He would pay a bonus to the player who broke up a double play at second. He would put catchers in full gear and hit line drives at them from forty feet. "He absolutely scared them to death at first," says the Pirates' Keller. "It was his way of getting their attention." Once he had their attention, it was a different story. "He had incredible patience and compassion," says Rickey. "You just didn't see him blow up with players, just as he didn't with his own children."

Rickey tells the story of Doug Frobel, a former Pirates outfielder who played for Scripture at Charleston, South Carolina, in 1978. Rickey had made a post-game dinner appointment with the manager, and he remembers watching as Charleston lost a heartbreaker in which Frobel failed at the plate and mishandled several balls in the outfield. Afterward, Rickey waited outside the locker room for thirty minutes before asking a departing player if Scripture was ready. "No, he's out on the field," he was told.

Outside, the stadium lights were still on—a costly indulgence for a minor-league club—and Scripture, in uniform, was kneeling in front of home plate, soft-tossing baseballs to Frobel, who tried to drive them to the opposite field.

"I just sat and watched," Rickey says. "There were about a hundred balls in the bucket, and when they had exhausted it, they walked out and picked them all up, talking softly. Then they came back and started again. And over the next half-hour, I watched them go through three buckets of baseballs.

"Now it gets to be about a quarter till twelve, the lights are still on. Bill picks up his fungo bat, sends Frobel into the outfield and starts hitting high fly balls, as only Bill can hit them. Frobel missed a lot of them, and Bill walked out to talk some more. When he brought the bucket back and started to hit another hundred, I finally yelled, 'Bill, are we going to dinner?' Bill looked at me, and without a word he waved Frobel in and turned off the lights."

Ultimately, Frobel went on to accomplish what Scripture never did: He reached the majors. Rickey gives partial credit to the manager. "I never saw anybody with that kind of willingness to work with a struggling player. That he was missing dinner was of no concern to Bill; the cost of the lights was of no concern to him. Everybody talks about the crazy things, but what attracted me to Billy Scripture was the other stuff."

Willie Wilson, the Royals center fielder, played for Scripture at Jacksonville in 1976. "He had the most impact of all the coaches and managers I've had," Wilson says. "He was a wild man, but he never did anything to show off. He did it to teach you."

Wilson tells this story: In August of that year, Wilson was on the verge of quitting baseball. An injury had put him on crutches for two weeks, and now that he was back, Scripture wasn't playing him. After sitting out the first game of a doubleheader, Wilson had had enough. "I yanked my uniform off and drove home, listening to the game on the radio." Realizing that he had acted rashly, Wilson changed his mind and drove back to the ballpark, only to find that Scripture had put his uniform in the washing machine.

"He made me put my uniform on wet," Wilson recalls. "I sat on one end of the bench while he sat on the other end with this funny smile on his face. And then after the game he took me down the left-field line for a talk."

During the talk Wilson learned why he wasn't playing: Scripture was keeping him healthy because the Royals were about to call him up for a September trial. "I still look up to Billy," Wilson says. "I never really had a father, but if I had a father, I'd want him to be like Billy Scripture."

Scripture hasn't forgotten that long-ago conversation. He says he remembers everything about it—the exact spot where they stood, the wind, the lights, the temperature, everything. "I remember looking Willie right in the eye and saying, 'Will, if you'll stay, you'll make a million dollars someday.' He was in Double A, strugglin' his ass off, but I had a lot of faith in Willie as a person."

Scripture shakes his head. "I loved my players. That bull—you can't get close to the players? Hey, I *argued* for 'em, I *fought* for 'em. Your successful manager always has a way of letting the players know, 'Hey, I'm for *you.* I'm here to help you.' "

This last is spoken back in the gun club shellhouse, late Saturday night. The shooters are asleep in hotel rooms or watching TVs in campers behind the clubhouse. Scripture sits on a case of shells and lights up another thin cigar. "I'll tell you what it would take to get me back in baseball," he says, tossing the match out the door. "It would take a struggling organization that wanted to turn around its minor-league system. I'd just like a hell of a good challenge. I'd like to take a can of worms and piece it together." The distant look in his eye suggests that it will never happen.

"It's a horse—— statement to say you're the last of a dying breed, but I played like there was no tomorrow. I ran into walls, fell into dugouts. It didn't matter *when* I played, *where* I played, how hot or how cold. I played baseball for the sheer effing love of playing. I always felt like if I'd had some ability, I would have been a hell of a ballplayer."

Scripture gets to his feet. "That kind of talk—it's just running away from getting old."

Outside in the dark, he takes a deep breath and looks up at the stars. "I enjoy the hell out of what I'm doing now," he says. "I love it." He crosses the grass to a light tower and pulls a switch. Light floods a narrow patch of skeet field—the spokes and wheel of sidewalk, brown grass littered with target fragments, the squat shape of the trap house. The paint on the sidewalls is green, like ballpark paint. The light is ballpark light.

Scripture looks around and nods contentedly. "It's just like walkin' into an empty ballpark, isn't it? Nothin' left but the pigeons and the popcorn."

STADIUM INFORMATION

Osceola County Stadium
1000 Osceola Blvd.
Kissimmee, FL 34744
(407) 933-5500

How long at present location: Six years
Capacity: 5,000
Dimensions: 330 feet down lines, 380-foot alleys, 410 feet to center
Directions: From I-4, exit on Highway 192 East; stadium is approximately twelve miles on left, just past fairgrounds. From Florida Turnpike, exit on Highway 192 West. Stadium is approximately one mile on right.
Parking: Paved, $2.00.

It was the Houston Astros' 1985 move to Kissimmee (pronounced "Kiss-SIM-ee") that touched off this latest round of stadium-jumping by clubs lusting for more ball diamonds and hunks of Florida real estate, so the purist may approach Osceola Stadium primed for disapproval. Happily, neither the ballpark nor the practice fields were constructed with an anti-fan bias. The stadium is surrounded by palm trees and enclosed by a high, grassy berm, thereby minimizing the sun-baked fan's exposure to sun-baked concrete. There is a grassy area down the right-field line where restless youngsters can chase foul balls and roughhouse without bothering the adults. The players stroll onto the field from a gate down the left-field line, contributing to the informality.

Kissimmee, the town, is another matter altogether. Highway 192, which runs past the stadium, is the principal funnel into the Disney development, and driving it can be a bear. When Walt Disney first turned his bulldozers loose in Florida, 192 was a two-lane highway. Ever since, the highway has been in the process of being widened, with bumper-to-bumper traffic the inevitable result. Sections of 192, by now, are about eighteen lanes wide, but traffic still crawls among the orange barrels, traffic cones, and heavy machinery. One suspects that traffic would move freely if the traffic experts would just stop widening the damn thing and get rid of the barrels, but of course that will never happen.

The other thing to know about Kissimmee is that everything is alligators. You can get alligator chowder, alligator-jaw hats, and inflatable rubber alligators, and your kids can crawl on alligator statuary, and you can pay to see alligators jump for snacks, and there's probably an alligator dating service if your taste runs in that direction.

What you can't get in Kissimmee is back to the Super 8 Motel from Disney World before your kids start fighting.

Ticket Information: box $7; reserved $6; general admission $4. Orders accepted after January 1. MasterCard, VISA, check, or money order are acceptable forms of payment. To order by mail, write: Spring Training Tickets, Osceola County Stadium, P.O. Box 422979, Kissimmee, FL 34742-2979. To order by phone, call Ticketmaster, (407) 839-3900. For ticket information only, (407) 933-2520.

Autograph Opportunities: "This is the easiest place in Florida to get autographs, even better than Port Charlotte," says Don Stevens, a collector from Orlando. "There are several spots where you can walk right up to the players." Kevin Kelly of Tampa agrees: "It seems like the Astros go out of their way to be accommodating to the fans." Stevens and Kelly recommend waiting in the parking lot outside the team offices and clubhouse, which are in a building some distance from the stadium on the left-field side. It's also easy to get players to stop on the sidewalk as they approach the field gate behind third base.

Hotels: The team hotel is the Hyatt Orlando at I-4 and U.S. 192 East, 6375 West Irlo Bronson Memorial Highway, Kissimmee, FL 34741; (407) 396-1234. It's on the large side: four swimming pools and an in-house shopping center. If you like your Hyatts even bigger, try the nearby Hyatt Regency Grand Cypress Hotel in Lake Buena Vista, where the main swimming pool is tricked up with waterfalls, grottoes, and a swaying suspension bridge. There's also a twenty-one-acre lake, a white sand beach, and an eighteen-hole, Jack Nicklaus-designed golf course. And if *that* isn't big enough, you can check into Marriott's contribution to Disney lodging: Marriott's Orlando World Center, which has ten restaurants and lounges distributed amid its many fairways, tennis courts, pools, and spas.

Mom-and-pop motels are plentiful on the neon-and-gravel stretch of U.S. 192 west of the ballpark. It's here also that you'll find oversized branches of the chains—Comfort Inn, Econo Lodge, Days Inn, etc. The ambiance is truck-stop traditional, but the room rates are low, particularly as you get away from Disney World and closer to the ballpark.

Area Attractions

• **Theme parks.** Kissimmee bills itself as "Gateway to the Worlds," which is a cute way of saying that U.S. 192 West runs right by Disney's door. (See "Central Florida's Black Hole of Tourism," p. 57.)
• Alligators at **Gatorland Zoo**, between Orlando and Kissimmee on U.S. 17-92-441. If you enjoyed the alligator feeding-frenzy in the movie *Indiana Jones and the Temple of Doom*, this is your chance to meet those gators face-to-face and maybe get some autographs. More than 5,000 bad-complected specimens, including trained gators jumping for handouts (and hands). Open daily from 8:00 A.M. Adults $5.40, children under twelve $3.95, children under three free.
• **Tupperware International Headquarters**, five miles south of the Florida Turnpike on Orlando's South Orange Blossom Trail (U.S. 17-92-441). Tours of this spectacular corporate headquarters are conducted Monday through Friday, 9:00 A.M. to 4:00 P.M. Tell them Buddy Biancalana sent you.

THE TEN QUOTATIONS MOST OFTEN ATTRIBUTED TO ASTROS COACH YOGI BERRA:

1. "It ain't over till it's over."
2. "It's *déjà vu* all over again."
3. "If people don't want to come to the park, nobody's going to stop 'em."
4. "Nobody ever goes there anymore—it's too crowded." (Said about a popular restaurant.)
5. "Culture demands continuous sublimation; it thereby weakens Eros, the builder of culture." (Also attributed to Herbert Marcuse.)
6. "You can observe a lot just by watching."
7. "I want to thank everybody for making this night necessary." (At a dinner in his honor.)
8. "If you can't imitate him, don't copy him."
9. "In baseball, you don't know nothing."
10. "I could've probably said that." (In reply to whether he actually ever uttered the nine previous statements.)

Restaurants, Lounges, and Dives: "There's a bar in Kissimmee that's one of the all-time great places," says Neil Hohlfeld of the *Houston Chronicle.* "It's called the Big Bamboo, and it's an oasis in all that junk out at the 535 turnoff on Highway 192. They play big-band music and it's got everything that Bruce the Bartender has accumulated in thirty years hanging from the ceiling. Larry Dierker and I pretty much discovered the place, but you see guys from Minnesota and Kansas City hanging out, too. And Disney people. It's packed with Disney people when they get off the three-to-eleven shift. Bruce must have over a thousand Disney badges; when employees leave Disney, they leave their badges at the Bamboo. Bruce the bartender, he's a hell of a guy. He's a pharmacist who moved down from Michigan, and now he's got this place. It's on Bamboo Lane—I think he put the sign up himself—and they've had to build around him, every cheap restaurant and franchise you can imagine. He's resisted every effort to sell out. I'm sure he's turned down millions of dollars, and for that I'm glad."

That's about it for Kissimmee, but there are scads of places in Orlando proper. "The number one place is Villa Rosa," says Twins media-relations director Tom Mee. "It's an Italian place that serves steaks, seafood, and spaghetti, and they put a big antipasto salad in the middle of the table. All the drinks are doubles—I found out the hard way."

Another former Twins hangout is Lee and Rick's Oyster Bar and Seafood House, which is near the Bay Hill Resort and Country Club. During the Nestle Invitational you see tournament golfers like Craig Stadler and Fuzzy Zoeller eating oysters by the bucket and dining on smoked mullet. Orlando also has its own Bubble Room,

which has a little train that chugs around near the ceiling and a booth made out of an old Chrysler . . . not to mention outstanding pastries.

"There's a beautiful French place that everybody calls the Mason Jar," says Mee, "but its real name is *Maison et Jardin.* It means 'house and garden.' At this restaurant they give the women a menu with no prices on it! It'll easily cost you fifty dollars apiece without drinks."

Chamber of Commerce: 320 E. Monument Ave., Kissimmee, FL 34741; (407) 847-3174. Also, Orlando Chamber of Commerce, 75 Ivanhoe Blvd., P.O. Box 1234, Orlando, FL 32802; (407) 425-1234. Also, the Orlando-Orange County Convention and Visitors Bureau, 8445 International Dr., Orlando, FL 32819; (407) 363-5871.

Spring Training Sites: 1962–63, Apache Junction, AZ; 1964–84, Cocoa, FL; 1985–present, Kissimmee.

Won–Lost Record/Attendance:

Year	Record	Attendance
1989	10–22	66,227
1988	17–15–1	64,412
1987	13–15	64,185
1986	9–18–1	56,760
1985	14–17	54,199

CENTRAL FLORIDA'S BLACK HOLE OF TOURISM

You don't have to be a sucker for conspiracy theories to suspect that some Goldfinger-type villain, headquartered under Orlando, is trying to lure all the world's tourists to Central Florida for some diabolical purpose. What's baffling is why this evil character thinks each tourist will need two hotel rooms. In Orlando, you don't say, "I'm staying at the Econo Lodge." You say, "I'm staying at the International Drive Econo Lodge, south of Sand Lake Road, west side of the street, just past the fire hydrant." That way, your friends won't look for you at some other Econo Lodge two blocks away.

There are so many hotels here that recommending any one is like trying to choose a really nice grain of sand at the beach. Fortunately, they tend to cluster (the hotels, that is), and the baseball tourist can select his hotel from one of several groups:

• Lake Buena Vista/Disney World. There are about a dozen major resort hotels on or near Disney property, including the Polynesian Village, the Contemporary Hotel, the Grand Floridian Beach Resort (on Buena Vista Lagoon), the Hilton at Disney World, and two mammoth hostelries, the Hyatt Regency Grand Cypress Hotel and Marriott's Orlando World Center.

• International Drive. Also known as Florida Center, this long strip just off I-4 has dozens of hotels, from modestly priced chains to elegant resorts, as well as a wealth of restaurants. Among the nicer properties are the Orlando Marriott Inn (lagoons, tennis courts, pools, and a good outdoor spa), the Peabody Orlando (featuring, at 11:00 A.M. daily, Peabody's famous "parade of quacking ducks"), the Radisson Inn & Justus Aquatic Center (Olympic-size swimming pool, hydraulic roof, high-diving boards, underwater observation room), and the Stouffer Resort at Sea World (massive atrium, gazebos, aviary, plaster dolphins).

• Highway 192/Kissimmee. Dozens of budget motels here, from big chains to mom-and-pops. Many have good views of miniature golf and the mini-car race tracks.

• Airport area. No games and glamour here, but plenty of rooms. Tell the kids you're going to a "tired businessman theme park."

• Downtown. The Harley Hotel has a good view of Lake Eola, but there are several other downtown hotels convenient to the Twins' Tinker Field.

Central Florida's theme parks are world-famous, which is no reason not to go. Here is a list of the biggest attractions:

• Mousetown. The 27,000-acre Disney complex now includes the unsurpassed Magic Kingdom, EPCOT Center, and the recently opened Disney-MGM Studios Theme Park, a $400 million production facility/theme park. "It's the largest theme park run by actors or cartoon characters," Bob Hope said at the opening, "unless you count Washington, D.C." For information and ticket prices, call (407) 824-4321.

• Sea World, 7007 Sea World Drive at the I-4 Sea World exit. This is the world's largest marine-life theme park, and it's operated by the same people who ran Boardwalk and Baseball, which is probably why Shamu the Killer Whale's swimming pool is called "Shamu Stadium." Lots of sharks. Adults $25.40, children three to twelve $21.15, children under three free. Call (407) 351-3600.

• Wet 'n' Wild, 6200 International Drive. Kamikaze slides, surf pools, white-water slideways, speedboats, and the Bonzai Boggan water roller coaster. Open daily, 10:00 A.M. to 6:00 P.M., from mid-February to November. Adults $13, children three to thirteen $11, children under three free. Call (407) 351-3200.

• Universal Studios Tour. This East Coast version of the popular California studio tour opened in May, 1990.

1001
NACHT

STADIUM INFORMATION
Baseball City Stadium
Interstate 4 and U.S. 27
Baseball City, FL 33844

How long at present location: Three years
Capacity: 7,000
Dimensions: 330 feet down lines, 385-foot alleys, 410 feet to center
Directions: Exit I-4 at Highway 27, south of Disney World. You're there.
Parking: Theme-park-size paved lots.

The Hurricane roller coaster was auctioned off in July. So was the kiddie ferris wheel. Somebody who needed a dance floor bought the "Dance U.S.A." building and drove away with it. Other buyers carried off everything from carnival supplies to office equipment.

Boardwalk and Baseball: *R.I.P.* The Royals now train at Boarded-up and Baseball, the best little out-of-the-way truck stop in the Grapefruit League.

All along, what saved this stunning complex from the utter sterility of the Mets' Versailles at Port St. Lucie was the Coney Island–style amusement park next door. The rackety roar of the wood roller coaster and the din of teenagers screaming as they plunged to almost certain death brought smiles to a grown-up, and it was hard to dislike a place where kids walked around with cotton candy in their pusses and balloons tied to their wrists.

Alas, Busch Entertainment Corporatioin, the "family entertainment subsidiary" of the big beer company that owns the St. Louis Cardinals, bought B&B as part of a theme park package and quickly shut it down. That leaves Baseball City as the Yuma of Florida spring baseball, a foreign legion outpost that only a confirmed Royals fan would pass Disney World to visit.

The ballpark itself represents a lost opportunity. The original plans for Boardwalk and Baseball called for a period baseball stadium—a new "old" park, as it were. If built as visualized by the architects, the Royals might now be playing in a ballpark with flag-topped cupolas, barrel vaults, and old-timey colonnades. Unfortunately, the chairman of the board of Harcourt Brace Jovanovich, the publishing giant that built Boardwalk and Baseball, deep-sixed the plan in favor of a more modern design. "We tried to second-guess the chairman," says one former B&B staffer, "and we didn't guess right."

Too bad. The decision to make the new stadium "major league" in every way, right down to the underground tunnels, heightens the fan's sense that he is at a baseball zoo. He can wander about on the concrete paths and peer through fences and over moats at ballplayers frolicking in their natural habitat, but there is no danger that one of the players will get loose.

Another consequence of the Royals' move from Ft. Myers to the Haines City interchange is that they play to apathetic crowds. "The majority of the people at Terry Park were Royals fans," says John Schuerholz, the Royals general manager. "This area is the vacation capital of the United States. The fans are here to see baseball, not necessarily to see us."

> "Spring training in Orlando seems forced. In Ft. Myers I used to drive over the bridge at five o'clock and see the sun going down over Sanibel Island. Now I fight the Disney traffic back to Orlando and stay in a hotel overlooking the interstate."
>
> —Fred White, Royals broadcaster

But don't imagine for a minute that the Royals would trade their new facility for the old one at Terry Park, no matter how much they loved the Shell Coast beaches. Says Schuerholz: "There used to be times in Ft. Myers we had to leave before the sun came up, be three hours on the bus, play a three-hour ballgame, then spend another three hours back on the bus. Six hours on the bus and you arrive again in the dark. We really couldn't get as much work done."

Adds a former Royal: "There's something to be said for hot water in the showers, too."

Ticket Information: box $7.50; reserved $6.50; stadium concourse $5 (day of game only); general admission bleacher and grass seating $4 (day of game only). Tickets may be ordered by writing to Baseball City Stadium and Sports Complex, 300 Stadium Way, Davenport, FL

33837. Phone orders will be taken after November 26 at (813) 424-2424.

Autograph Opportunities: Poor. Front-row railings are fine, but everything else—clubhouse exits, player parking, batting cages, and practice fields—are fenced in. "The Royals have the toughest park in Florida, no question," says Tom Bunevich. "A couple of years ago, we were sitting by a fence, and a guy in a golf cart came out and said, 'You can't sit here.' " Another collector says: "I went by there once. It's crazy, it's ridiculous."

The players aren't bad, though. Collector Dave Stahl of Kansas City says that second-baseman Frank White is "number one, by far" among the Royals. "He's always smiling. It doesn't matter how many people are waiting, he always says, 'No problem.' He visits with you. He shows an interest."

Another collector, who wouldn't give his name, said, "I put George Brett with the worst. He'll sign sometimes, but he's real unpleasant about it. He won't look at you, and then he sort of shoves it back."

Brett responds: "People who ask for autographs don't understand what a burden it is sometimes when you have to sign a hundred of them in a day. You go through your mail and get fifty letters a day, and people write back and say, 'I wrote you a letter and you didn't send me back a card,' or 'You didn't sign my birthday card.' And it's just frustrating. You sign one picture for everybody in the stands, and suddenly everybody in the stands has *two* pictures." Didn't Brett collect autographs when he was a kid? "Never. My parents didn't like it if I stayed out till one o'clock."

Team Hotel: The Sonesta Village Hotel, 10000 Turkey Lake Road, Orlando, FL 32819; (407) 352-8051. The Sonesta is a richly landscaped, condominium-style hotel about twenty miles from Boardwalk and Baseball. Several chain motels are right on the Baseball City strip (Highway 27), but none are especially recommended. A few Royals people and media types have stayed across the highway at the Holiday Inn ("Not the worst place I've ever stayed," says one TV reporter, grudgingly), but repeat bookings are rare. Alan Eskew, who follows the Royals for the *Topeka Capital Journal,* covered the '89 spring training from a high-rise condominium on a lake in Winter Haven. ("It was very nice . . . but I'd rather be back in Ft. Myers on the beach.") In their first year at B&B, the Royals made the Stouffer Orlando Resort at Sea World their headquarters, and many Kansas Citians fell in love with that hotel's huge atrium lobby full of gilded clocks, Victorian birdcages, and spectacular plantings. For other Orlando-area hotels, see "Central Florida's Black Hole of Tourism," p. 57.

Area Attractions

• **None.**

• Okay, practically none. There is quality golf nearby at the **Grenelefe Resort & Conference Center** on State Rd. 546. This four-diamond resort gets good marks from both *Golf* and *Golf Digest* magazines, and children under eighteen get to stay free with parents. Call (800) 237-9549. (George Brett, when asked what he shot in a round of golf a few years ago: "Three over, I think. Over one house, over one patio, over one swimming pool. Yeah, three over.")

In the Orlando area:

• **Theme parks.** Disney World, EPCOT Center, Sea World, Disney–MGM Studios, Universal Studios, *et al.* and *ad nauseam.* See "Central Florida's Black Hole of Tourism," p. 57.

• **Lake Eola.** This lovely tree-lined lake in downtown Orlando has undergone extensive improvements, making it one of the South's nicer urban parks. For information about walking tours of the lake and downtown Orlando, call (407) 843-7463.

• **The Elvis Presley Museum** is on the second floor of a building on International Drive in Orlando, a short walk from Morrison's Cafeteria. If that interests you, that's all you need to know.

Restaurants, Lounges, and Dives: "Haines City is still the same," reports Royals beat writer Alan Eskew. "You either eat at Sonny's barbecue or you don't eat at all."

Not surprisingly, hungry Royals look north to Orlando. Royals manager John Wathan loved an oom-pah place called the Bavarian Schnitzel House, where a couple of guys called "The Sauerkrauts" played twelve-foot alpine horns and told jokes while the patrons pigged out on German food. Unfortunately, the Schnitzel House, like Boardwalk and Baseball, is no more. Wathan has moved on to the Fisherman's Deck, just off I-4 in Buena Vista Village. "You can see it from the freeway, " says Wathan. "The swordfish is outstanding and they've got a good raw bar." Pressed for other restaurants, Wathan looks reflective. "What's that one with the big gold arch?"

Independence Examiner sportswriter Bill Althaus recommends Jonathan's on International Drive. "I had scallops. They must have given me thirty scallops, and every one was as big as a silver dollar."

The author recommends the Chelsea restaurant in the Orlando Marriott Hotel on International Drive—great lunch and dinner buffets at a reasonable price. If you have room for dessert, cross the street and have some lime Jell-O at Morrison's Cafeteria.

The best sports bar? According to Kansas City sportscaster Dave Stewart, it's the J.B. Sports Bar on Kirkman Road. "God, it was huge and it was packed and they had every helmet, hat, and pennant in existence. A friend of mine who lives in Orlando says it's where all the locals go. If you like eating finger foods while watching a ball game and having a cold one, that's the best place I've seen anywhere."

Chamber of Commerce: None.

Spring Training Sites: 1969–87, Ft. Myers, FL; 1988–present, Baseball City.

Won-Lost Record/Attendance:

Year	Record	Attendance
1989	16–11–2	85,163
1988	17–13	89,999
1987	12–13	55,489
1986	11–14–1	65,354
1985	12–15	63,928

BUDDY BIANCALANA'S TOP 10 PLACES FOR DAVID LETTERMAN TO VISIT ON HIS FLORIDA VACATION

10. "Big Daddy" Don Garlits' Museum of Drag Racing, Ocala

9. Spongeorama, Tarpon Spring

8. Xanadu, Home of the Future, Orlando-Kissimmee

7. Water Skiing Hall of Fame, Winter Haven

6. The Tragedy in U.S. History Museum, St. Augustine

5. Butterfly World, Ft. Lauderdale

4. Waltzing Waters Show, Naples-Fort Myers

3. Bellm's Cars and Music of Yesterday, Sarasota

2. "Gator Jumperoo" at Gatorland Zoo, Orlando-Kissimmee

and finally, the Number One place for David Letterman to visit on his Florida vacation . . . (drum roll)

1. THE GALLERY OF HISTORIC FOOD CONTAINERS AT THE TUPPERWARE INTERNATIONAL HEADQUARTERS, ORLANDO!

An Interview with Royals Groundskeeper George Toma

NOTE: Toma specifically refers to himself and others of his profession as "groundkeepers."

Q: How do you keep yourself busy this time of year? *(Asked with a smile)*
A: Are you serious? We have forty-two pitching mounds in this complex, and we have fifty home plates. There are eight hitting tunnels. Everybody thinks a groundkeeper spends all his time on the grass, but in baseball the grass is secondary. The infield, pitching mound, and home plate come first.

Q: What do you do to maintain the mounds?
A: At Ft. Myers, where city employees took care of the field most of the time, we had to rebuild the mounds and the sliding pits every spring. The pitchers want it just right, they don't want a mound that's too soft or too hard or full of holes. Here, we've got a great groundkeeper all year in Ed Mangum, and he takes care of that. But I believe that dirt dies. You've got to put life in it again.

Q: In Kansas City you mix sand from river bottoms and clay from Georgia and various soils from all over the country to get a dirt that's just right. Where do you get your dirt for Boardwalk and Baseball?
A: In Florida it's hard to get good clay. At Ft. Myers we used to get it out of Georgia. This year we're getting our clay from a Plant City brickyard, the clay used to make bricks. Last year, we'd check where they were building golf courses around the Tampa area. They'd hit marl—that's a mixture of clays and shells—and we'd put that in front of the rubber. Right now, we're getting our infield soil from Hollister, Florida. You just have to look around. The Twins used to bring their own dirt down from Minnesota, and the Phillies would bring dirt down from Delaware. In Kansas City we're lucky, I just go down below the Chiefs practice field with a bucket and get all I want.

Q: Do groundskeepers fiddle with the mounds to help their team?
A: When I was a young groundkeeper they did. The visitors' bullpen might be flat, for example, and when the pitcher came into the game and warmed up on a fifteen-inch mound, that threw him off. I remember Catfish Hunter when he pitched for the Yankees, he thought we were fooling around with the mound at Royals Stadium. During the playoffs, the kids on our ground crew would psych him out by asking him if he'd brought his putty knife.

Sometimes your pitchers would like to see you cheat a little bit, make the slope steeper or something like that. But you can't.

Q: Does that mean that every mound in the big leagues is identical?
A: Yes and no. They're all built to conform to league rules. It has to be exactly sixty feet six inches from the base of home plate to the foot of the rubber, and the rubber has to be ten inches above the plate. The flat spot on top of the mound, what we call the "table," has to extend eighteen inches to each side of the rubber, which is precisely six inches by twenty-four inches. And the slope must drop in one-inch increments, one inch per foot. But no two mounds are exactly the same because the dirt is always a little different. Pitchers tailor them with their spikes and heels, and they just wear differently according to who's pitching. They don't make pitching rubbers like they used to, either. When I came to the major leagues in 1957, the rubbers didn't tear up or buckle on you. They used to be six inches of solid rubber. Now, with all our technology, they don't make 'em solid any more. They're hollow filled with concrete. Same with home plates—rubber over plywood.

Royals groundskeeper George Toma

Q: How do spring-training fields today compare with the fields of, say, ten years ago?
A: Much better. There used to be a lot of bad fields down here. Some teams wouldn't take infield practice because their managers didn't want players to develop bad habits or get hurt. The reason there were so many bad fields is because they weren't maintained properly. I made a lot of people mad by blaming the Florida ground crews, but sometimes you've got to step on people's toes. They'd make an excuse like, "The dirt's no good." I'd say, "It's not the dirt. It's the man that works the dirt." And that's the truth. John Verdi, the California Angels groundkeeper, told me he went to spring training one time, looked out his motel window, and saw one of the city workers dragging the infield with a pickup truck. And the guy went right over second base with the drag!

Q: I've heard you say that cheap groundskeeping is a false economy in an age when ballplayers make fabulous salaries.
A: That's exactly right. These clubs have so much money tied up in their players, yet they'll try to cut corners on maintaining the field. What happens? The players get hurt and can't play, and the club loses money all around. That puts a lot of pressure on the groundkeeper. I remember in Ft. Myers one time, Doc Meyer and Al Zych were walking by third base, and one of them said, "Make sure that base is perfect, 'cause that's our franchise." Of course, they meant George Brett. The next day, a bad hop hit George right in the jaw and knocked some teeth out.

Q: Are you still the best groundskeeper in baseball?
A: *(Shaking his head)* I'm sixty years old, I'm over the hill. The greatest today, in the big leagues, is Jimmy Anglia of the Texas Rangers. Nobody can shine that guy's shoes. They should use his fields for pool tables. And Tommy Burns, the guy who does the Rangers' field at Port Charlotte, he's very, very good.

Q: I get the impression that you scout groundskeepers in spring training, just like the baseball men scout players.
A: I do, because teams are always calling me up to recommend somebody for a job. The Dodgers needed a new groundkeeper, and I told Tommy Lasorda to hire Al Hicks, a kid I used to yell at all the time. I said, "He's ready." There are others down here. Mike Hurd, he's over at Plant City. Barney Lopez.

And Ed Magnum, here at Boardwalk and Baseball, he'll be a major-league groundkeeper. You don't just judge a groundkeeper by how his field looks, but also by how many games are played on it. The stadium here has baseball every day, over four hundred games a year. Ed should have the worst field in Florida after that many games, but the root system here is eighteen to twenty-four inches deep. Some new stadiums have two inches or less! What Ed has done here, that's good groundkeeping.

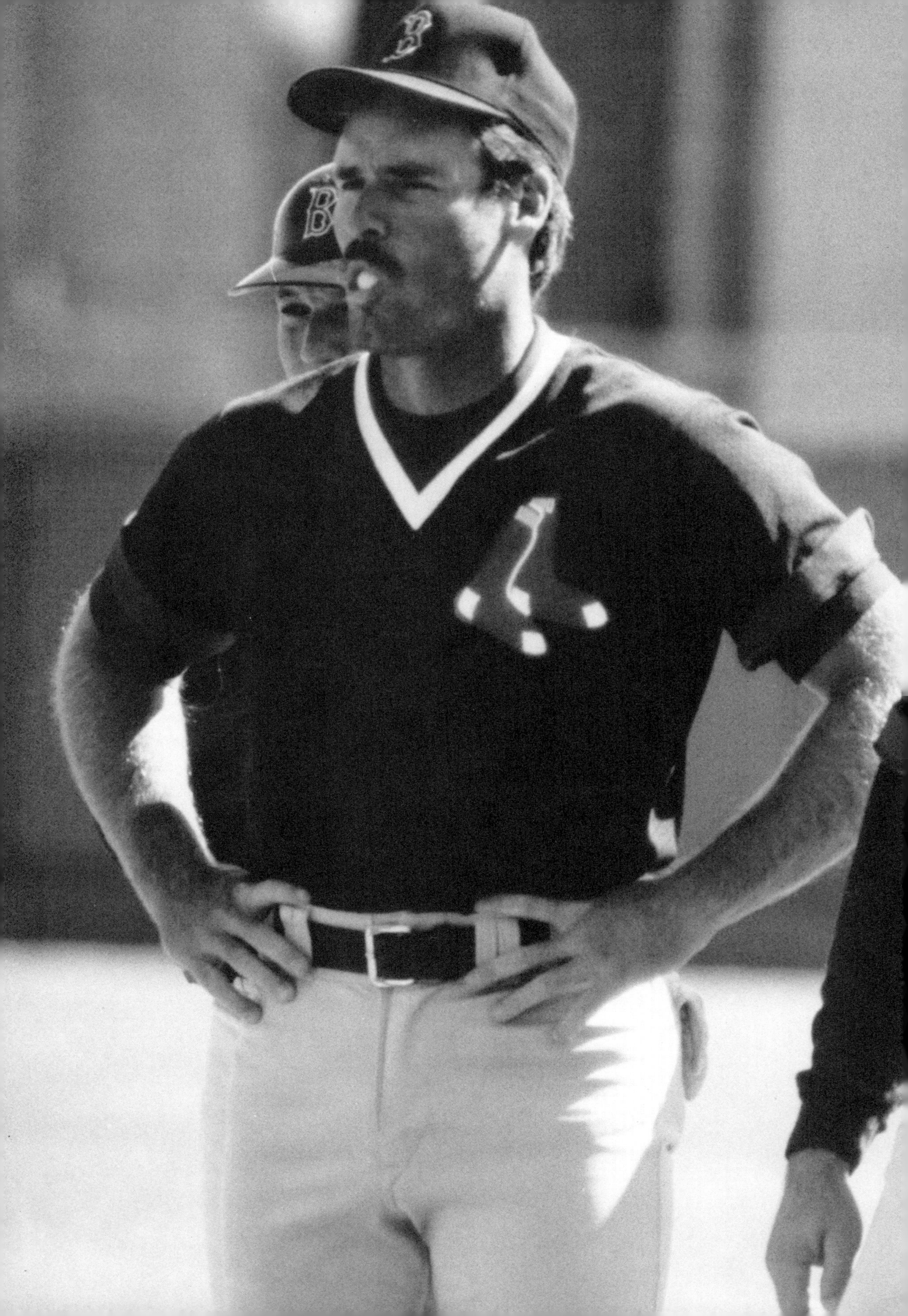

STADIUM INFORMATION

Chain O'Lakes Park
Cypress Gardens Boulevard
Winter Haven, FL 33880
(813) 293-3900

How long at present location: Twenty-four years
Capacity: 4,502
Dimensions: 340 feet down lines, 425 feet to center
Directions: From Tampa, take I-4 east to Exit 92 (Memorial Blvd.), make a right to Highway 655 to Eloise; turn left on U.S. 17; go one mile, turn right onto Cypress Gardens Blvd.; stadium is three miles on right. From Orlando, take I-4 West to U.S. 27 South at Baseball City; turn right on 544; travel to signal at post office and turn right; make next left to U.S. 17, follow to ballpark.
Parking: Large lot, mostly grass.

"The worst thing a sportswriter can be is a fan," Jimmy Cannon used to say. A sportswriter himself and a legend in New York until his death in 1973, Cannon cast a jaundiced eye on the work of most of his colleagues, particularly those who cheered from the press box. He believed a press box should be filled with "guys who neither love nor hate the sport and whose life is not wrapped up in the sport and who remember they are working newspapermen and not baseball people."

Cannon's words seemed prophetic spring before last when hordes of newshounds descended on Chain O'Lakes Park to cover the Wade Boggs–Margo Adams sex scandal. Day after day, the press pack surrounded Boggs or pitcher Oil Can Boyd or general manager Lou Gorman in the fenced-in Red Sox compound down the first-base line. While birds twittered in the trees overhead and bees buzzed lazily over the outfield grass, the principals in the controversy deftly fielded questions about . . . well, the birds and the bees. Gorman, at one point, threw up his hands and said, "I didn't know sex was a disease"—a line that probably made tabloid headlines in New England.

Winter Haven is one of the few camps where baseball writers rival the players as celebrities. Your true Red Sox fan will argue the merits of either of two lineups, that of the *Boston Globe* (Nick Cafardo, Dan Shaughnessy, Steve Fainaru, Mike Madden, Larry Whiteside, and Bob Ryan) or the *Boston Herald* (Joe Giuliotti, Mike Shalin, Gerry Callahan, Steve Harris, Tim Horgan, and George Kimball), and both sides will agree that Beantown lost a municipal treasure when Pete Gammons went to *Sports Illustrated.* Old-timers love to tell tales about the legendary "Colonel" Dave Egan of the *Boston Daily Record,* who attacked athletes with inquisitorial zeal in the 1930s and 1940s.

"The competition is very healthy and keeps us on our toes," says Cafardo, beat writer for the *Globe*. "The *Globe*'s a lot bigger than the *Herald,* but the *Herald* really works at it and they have good people. We certainly pay attention to what they're doing, and we're concerned if they have a good story that we missed."

The press room at Chain O'Lakes, not surprisingly, is one of spring baseball's best, a two-

> "To me, Winter Haven is the ultimate when it comes to Florida camps. If Chain O'Lakes Park lacks Fenway's Victorian angles, it has a greenness just as dazzling and a setting every bit as intimate. In red and green stands at Winter Haven, one gets the feeling of sitting on the front porch of a charming country home, with Jim Rice and Marty Barrett and Roger Clemens out playing on the front lawn.
>
> "Wander into Winter Haven, and you can unwind to the crack of bats by day and a lonesome train whistle by night. You want action, try football or go to Vegas."
>
> —William Gildea

room retreat with phones and workspace on one side of a wall and a homey dining room on the other, where the writers eat chowder in styrofoam cups with oyster crackers. From the end rail of the right field bleachers, you can watch the media types wander in and out through a screen door that looks like the entrance to a forest ranger's office. When they gather outside in a clump of eight or more, you know an impromptu press conference is about to begin.

"New England is baseball crazy, so we have to provide them a lot of copy every day," says Cafardo. "The beat writer has to write a feature a day and cover the news. The columnist writes something, a feature writer writes something, and sometimes we put a fourth guy on. We write a lot every day."

Actually, the Boggs episode was an anomaly: a compelling hard-news story from a spring training camp. More often, the Boston writers have to make a meal of very thin gruel, which spring training is, journalistically speaking. "Over the years," writes Ross Newhan of the *Los Angeles Times,* "baseball writers have hit journalistic lows stretching for six weeks of daily stories on .230 hitters predicting .300 seasons because of their new stances, control-plagued pitchers insisting that courses in positive thinking have cured their problems, and defensively inept teams returning to fundamentals, only to find later that they are still defensively inept."

Working newspapermen or baseball people? The jury is still out on that.

Ticket Information: lower box $6; upper box $5; general admission $4. Order by writing Chain O'Lakes Park, Cypress Gardens Blvd., Winter Haven, FL 33880, or call (813) 293-3900.

Autograph Opportunities: "The Red Sox are fairly nice," says Greg Hileman, owner of Hileman's Baseball Cards & Etc. in Winter Haven. "They're just hard to get to 'cause there's a fenced-in area where they drive up, and you're not allowed in. It's easier to get them down at the Holiday Inn."

"Generally, the older the park the easier," says Tampa collector Tom Bunevich, "with the exception of Winter Haven. I call that a concentration camp. It's virtually impossible. The players have to come to you, and that's a habit they haven't gotten into."

That leaves the stadium rails before and after the game, and some of the Red Sox make a point of coming over to sign. Wade Boggs, of all people, signed a lot of autographs while the Margo Adams controversy raged. It apparently helped his battered image; he got cheered on Opening Day, while Roger Clemens got booed.

Hotels: The team hotel is the Holiday Inn, 1150 Third St. SW, Winter Haven, FL 33880; (813) 294-4451. Most veteran players rent lakefront condos. There are a few dozen other motels with charming names like Millie's Motel, Garden Court Motel, and Banyan Beach Motel.

Area Attractions

• **Cypress Gardens**, County Road 540 at Cypress Gardens Blvd., Winter Haven, is your basic cypress swamp inhabited by show-off water-skiers and hoop-skirted Southern belles. Open daily from 8:00 A.M. to 6:00 P.M., shows at 10:00 A.M., 2:00 P.M., and 4:00 P.M. Adults $17.50, children three to eleven $11.50, others free. Call (813) 324-2111.

• **Chain O'Lakes Boat Tours.** The pontoon boats leave from lakes near downtown Winter Haven. Includes a view of the Cypress Gardens Ski Show.

• **Fishing and Boating.** The area's fresh-water lakes, rivers, and canals are noted for black bass, chain pickerel, bream, perch, redfinned pike, sunshine and striped bass, crappie, and catfish. A freshwater fishing license, required for anglers between the ages of fifteen and sixty-five, can be obtained at any sporting-goods store or at the American Legion Tag Office, Avenue M, N.W., just off Highway 17 in Winter Haven.

Restaurants, Lounges, and Dives: "Nick Christy's Sundown restaurant and Mario's Italian restaurant, those are the two top spots," says Joe Giuliotti of the *Boston Herald.* "Christy's is number one, I eat there ninety percent of the time. They have great steaks, and the seafood is flown in daily from New England. They have this thing, 'Greek spaghetti'—I never heard of that, but I tried it, and it's outstanding. And Nick's got grouper Athenian-style, which is made with some kind of Greek garlic, and it's unbelievable. I got hooked on that."

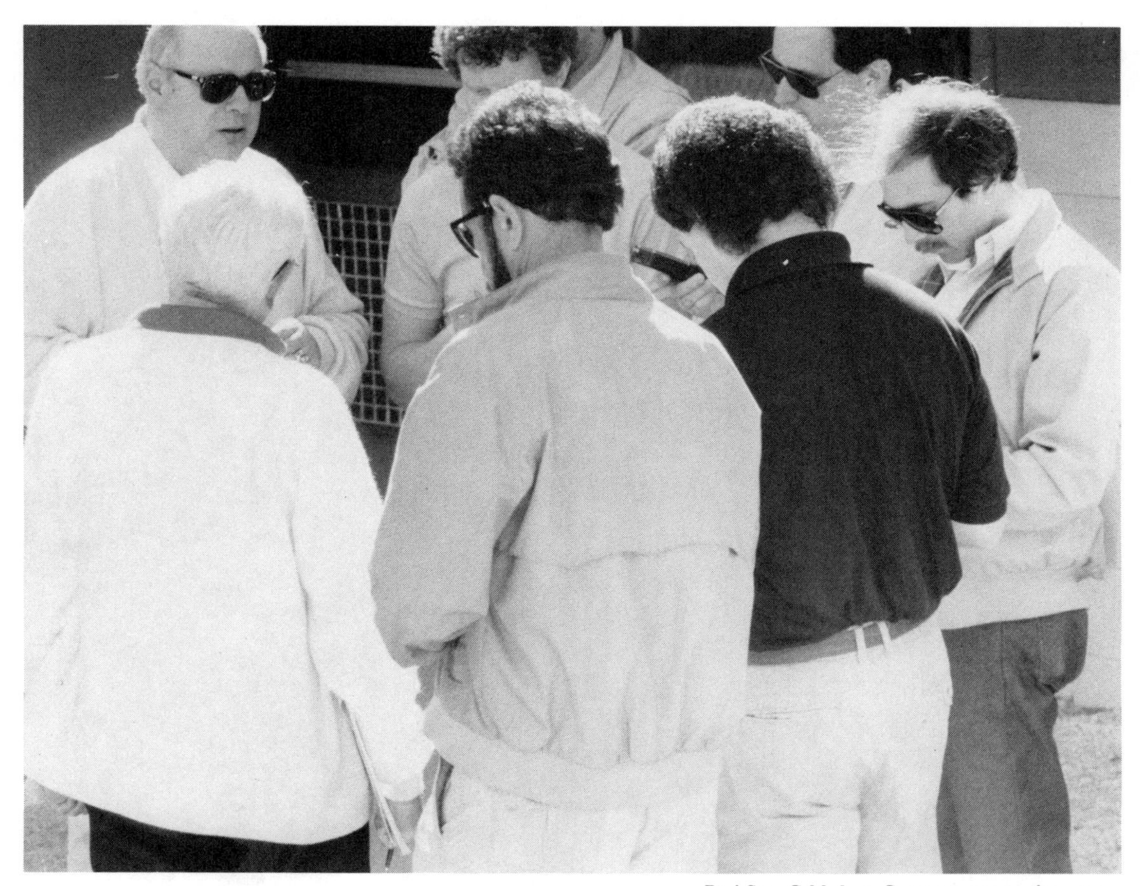

Red Sox G.M. Lou Gorman meets the press.

The Red Sox are hooked on Christy's, too—and why not, it's the only Mobil three-star restaurant next to the team hotel—but they also like Mario's, out near Cypress Gardens (plenty of Red Sox photos in the foyer), and Lombardo's, a fancy Italian place in an old house on Central Avenue ("That costs you a buck," says Giuliotti). Another place strong on atmosphere, Nostalgia, closed last year, but that was offset by the opening of a new Olive Garden restaurant on Cypress Gardens Boulevard, about a mile from the stadium.

Royals beat writer Alan Eskew says, "I went to a restaurant with the Boston writers where all the waiters and waitresses wore costumes. One of them was Peter Pan, I swear." We'd believe him, but he can't remember the name of the place.

"O'Brian's seems to be a very popular place in Winter Haven," says the *Globe*'s Cafardo. "It's mostly a ribs-type place similar to Friday's. It's always packed. I like the ribs there, and they have a great dessert, this chocolate brownie thing with ice cream on it. But the best place in town may be Hairston's. It used to be a little hole in the wall that hardly anybody knew about, but they moved into a place across the street from the Holiday Inn and near the stadium. It's kind of expensive, but well worth it. The finest dining in town."

"Gary's Harborside is also very good and close to the ballpark," says Giuliotti. "Very good oysters and shrimp."

After dinner, the younger players boogie over to Rumors, the nightclub at the Howard Johnson. "It's dead some nights, but it's really hopping on the weekends," says Cafardo. "There's usually a band." The older players don't boogie anywhere; they just glide into Christy's lounge.

Where do you go if you hope to catch a glimpse of Ted Williams? "I don't know," says Cafardo. "I've never seem him out."

Chamber of Commerce: 101 6th St. N.W., Winter Haven, FL 33881; (813) 293-2138.

Spring Training Sites: 1901, Charlottesville, VA; 1902, Augusta, GA; 1903–06, Macon, GA; 1907–08, Little Rock, AR; 1909–10, Hot Springs, AR; 1911, Redondo Beach, CA; 1912–18, Hot Springs, AR; 1919, Tampa, FL; 1920–23, Hot Springs, AR; 1924, San Antonio, TX; 1925–27, New Orleans; 1928–29, Bradenton, FL; 1930–31, Pensacola, FL; 1932, Savannah, GA; 1933–42, Sarasota, FL; 1943, Medford, MA; 1944, Baltimore; 1945, Pleasantville, NJ; 1946–58, Sarasota, FL; 1959–65, Scottsdale, AZ; 1966–present, Winter Haven.

Won-Lost Record /Attendance:

Year	Record	Attendance
1989	12–19–1	70,689
1988	17–13	60,747
1987	16–13	55,147
1986	12–16	40,741
1985	12–16–1	43,310

HOME OF
DETROIT TIGERS
Joker Marchant
STADIUM
TIGER BOX OFFICE
OPEN
9 5 MON SAT 12 4 SUN
TIGERTOWN

STADIUM INFORMATION

Marchant Stadium
Tigertown
1901 Lake Ave.
Lakeland, FL 33802
(813) 686-8075

How long at present location: Forty-five years
Capacity: 7,027
Dimensions: 340 feet down lines, 420 feet to center
Directions: From Orlando, take I-4 to Exit 16 (Memorial); east on Memorial Blvd. about three and a half miles to Lakeland Hills Blvd.; turn left and head north about one mile; stadium is on right. From Tampa, take *second* Highway 33 exit (Exit 19) and follow Highway 33 about two and a half miles; stadium is on left. From Winter Haven, take U.S. 92 west to Lakeland; at Lakeland Hills Blvd. (Highway 33), turn right. Stadium is about one mile on right.
Parking: Paved and grass and limitless, $2.00.

To visit Tigertown is to step into a scene from *War and Remembrance.* The complex is on an old air base, and asphalt and concrete stretches in all directions—perfect for air shows or jeep racing. Behind Hangar Number Two, the blue hangar, is Popovich Drive, named for George Popovich, who for many years ran the Tigers' minor-league clubhouse. The Tigers' spring-training offices are on the second floor of a military-style building. There's not much furniture; dark halls, curtainless windows, and boxes on the floor give the place the look of a temporary HQ. Which is strange, since the Tigers have trained at Lakeland since 1934.

Marchant Stadium is no prize. It's a big clunker of a place, underlandscaped and at the sun's mercy on a hot day. The bleachers down the left-field line, high and featureless, evoke a high school football stadium. The view from the high seats is undistinguished.

What Tigertown has going for it is Tiger fans. There is not a more partisan crowd in the Grapefruit League, and only the Cubs fans in Mesa, Arizona, are more devoted. Snowbirds with Tiger caps and Michigan license plates have been coming to Lakeland for so long that they tend to settle here when they retire. The Lakeland Area Chamber of Commerce throws a big barbecue for the Tigers every spring, and the line of fans waiting to get inside the hangar stretches a hundred yards across the tarmac.

And that makes Tigertown much better than the sum of its parts. Tradition counts.

Ticket Information: box $6.50; reserved $5.50; grandstand general admission $4 (1990 prices). Tickets can be ordered by mail after December 1, 1990. Until February 1, 1991, write: Spring Tickets, Detroit Baseball Club, Tiger Stadium, Detroit, MI 48216. After February 1, 1991, write: Spring Tickets, Detroit Baseball Club, P.O. Box 90187, Lakeland, FL 33804. No telephone orders taken. Cash and money orders, no credit cards accepted.

Autograph Opportunities: In addition to the usual railings, Tigertown autograph-seekers gather in large numbers in the parking lot out-

Dunes
LAS VEGAS
ATLAS
METALS

side the Tigers clubhouse door on the third-base side. "Lakeland is probably the second-best place to get autographs in Florida, because the players have to park in the parking lot and walk right by you," says Winter Haven collector Greg Hileman. "The only place that's easier is Dodgertown." Says Tampa collector Tom Bunevich: "The Tigers have a good setup, but the crowds have gotten so big. Last spring, I saw Alan Trammell turn people down. I thought the world was caving in on me. Trammell's always been the king, Mr. Nice Guy. He would stand after practice and sign, sign, sign."

Hotels: The team hotel is the Ramada Inn Lakeside, 910 E. Memorial Blvd., Lakeland, FL 33801; (813) 682-0101, and the best thing to recommend it is that it is within walking distance of Morrison's Cafeteria. There are two other Holiday Inns, one at Exit 19 on I-4 and one to the south, and a new Sheraton opened recently on South Florida Avenue.

Area Attractions

- **Madam Christine**, fortune-teller. For directions, consult billboards on U.S. 92 between Winter Haven and Lakeland.

Restaurants, Lounges, and Dives: "Around Lakeland, my favorite place is the Branch Ranch, just off Interstate 4 in Plant City," says Tigers play-by-play man Ernie Harwell. "It's Southern cooking. They have hot biscuits, country ham, steak, chicken, scalloped eggplant, chicken pot pie. That's a great place. Mrs. Branch was a schoolteacher who began the restaurant in her home. It's grown and grown, but they still keep the old home flavor. In 1968, Mrs. Branch was flown up to Detroit as a guest of the Tigers to see the World Series because so many of the club's people had eaten there."

"Actually, Lakeland isn't that bad an eating town," says Tom Gage of the *Detroit News*. "There are two good steakhouses, the Texas Cattle Company and Farmer Jones' Red Barn. There's an Olive Garden, which is pretty good Italian food. And they have a Chili's and a Bennigan's—the players go there a lot. This spring, John Lowe (of the *Detroit Free Press*) and I went to a little Italian place called Vito's. It's just a neighborhood, hole-in-the-wall-type place—nothing spectacular, just good, solid, dependable food. I like Chinese food, and my favorite in Lakeland is Chef Su. It's the only one in town that is consistent with spicy dishes, Szechwan style."

Chamber of Commerce: 35 Lake Morton Drive, Lakeland, FL 33801; (813) 688-8551.

Spring Training Sites: 1901, Detroit; 1902, Ypsilanti, MI; 1903–04, Shreveport, LA; 1905–07, Augusta, GA; 1908, Hot Springs, AR; 1909–10, San Antonio, TX; 1911–12, Monroe, LA; 1913–15, Gulfport, MS; 1916–18, Waxahachie, TX; 1919–20, Macon, GA; 1921, San Antonio, TX; 1922–26, Augusta, GA; 1927–28, San Antonio, TX; 1929, Phoenix; 1930, Tampa; 1931, Sacramento, CA; 1932, Palo Alto, CA; 1933, San Antonio, TX; 1934–42, Lakeland, FL; 1943–45, Evansville, IN; 1946–present, Lakeland.

> "By the time we arrived in Jacksonville, four of the fourteen players were reasonably sober, the rest were totally drunk. There was a fight every night, and the boys broke a lot of furniture. We played exhibitions during the day and drank most of the night."
>
> —Connie Mack on spring training with the 1888 Washington Senators, the first team to train in Florida

Alan Trammell tackles an 8-pt. meal.

Won–Lost Record/Attendance:

Year	Record	Attendance
1989	15–16–1	107,507
1988	11–19	90,858
1987	9–20	65,264
1986	18–11	86,764
1985	17–13	84,850

A Four-Time Gold Glove Shortstop with "Bad Hands"?

Alan Trammell, the Tigers' all-star shortstop, is neither a gourmet nor a gourmand. He is more of a gour-*blam.* (That's the sound made when a ballplayer gets up unexpectedly in a restaurant and upsets a waiter's fully loaded tray.) Former teammate Enos Cabell once dubbed Trammell "the world's worst eater." Another teammate, Marty Castillo, said, "I usually put plastic on the floor around Trammell's locker when he eats. I don't see how he gets nourishment. Nothing reaches his stomach."

Q: Are you still a bad eater?
Trammell: I've knocked over a few Coke glasses, yeah. I've got no explanation for it. On the baseball field I've got good hands, but at the dinner table I tend to spill things.

Q: Is it a question of concentration? Or just bad mechanics?
Trammell: I guess I get excited when I start talking, and my hands start moving. It's been that way since I was a kid. The way I look at it, when I'm ready to eat, I'm going to *eat.* If I get barbecue sauce on my shirt, I'm not going to worry about it.

Q: What are your favorite places to eat in Lakeland?
Trammell: Well, I've always liked the Red Barn, although I went from getting the two-pound porterhouse (TDD: 3)* to getting a large filet (TDD: 5). You get older, you learn not to eat as much red meat. I like asparagus (TDD: 3), and they've got nice asparagus, too. For Italian, my favorite place is Mario's. I get lasagna (TDD: 5), spaghetti (TDD: 7), or fettuccine Alfredo (TDD: 8). If I'm wearing something old, I go over to Sonny's Barbecue Pit and get either a chicken plate (TDD: 9) or the straight combo plate (TDD: 9).

***The Trammell Degree-of-Difficulty (TDD) Scale:**

1–2: Easy eating, no spills likely. (Dried apricots; raw carrots and celery; Life Savers)

3–4: Untidy, but spills confined to tablecloth or Trammell's lap. (Dinner rolls; salads; fried chicken; Rice-a-Roni; steaks; *poi;* popcorn)

5–6: Spills likely, stains on Trammell's clothes probable. (Casseroles; dips; soups; gravies; ice cream; fruit pies; beverages in open containers)

7–8: Spills inevitable, possible splashing of neighbors. (Pastas; Oriental noodle dishes; buffalo wings; grapefruit; broiled chicken; boiled shrimp in shell)

9–10: No one seated at table without a raincoat. (Lobster; crab legs; barbecued ribs or chicken; corn on the cob)

(Note: The Red Barn's filet mignon is two points higher than the porterhouse on the TDD Scale because toothpicks are inserted to hold the bacon to the steak during cooking.)

(Further note: Mario's went out of business shortly after Trammell's last meal there.)

STADIUM INFORMATION

Plant City Stadium
1900 South Park Road
Plant City, FL 33566
(813) 752-1878

How long at present location: Three years
Capacity: 6,700
Dimensions: 330 feet down lines, 375-foot alleys, 404 feet to center
Directions: From I-4, take Exit 14 (Park Road); go south on Park toward Plant City for two and a half miles; complex is on right. From Route 60, exit at James Redman Parkway (State Road-39); follow parkway four miles into Plant City; turn right at Park Road; stadium is one mile on left.
Parking: Some paved, plus large grass lot.

There was a lot of kidding about "Strawberry Fields Forever" when the Reds moved here from Tampa three years ago. Plant City farmers grow about four zillion of the little red yummies every year, and they celebrate spring with a ten-day Strawberry Festival. Berry nice.

Strangely, though, a stranger's dominant impression of Plant City is not of strawberries, but of trucks—specifically, Publix Supermarket trucks. They rumble past you singly and in caravans, on the interstate and on back roads, seemingly bound for all points of the compass. It turns out that an industrial park between Plant City and Lakeland is home to the Publix Distribution Center, where all the Publix dairy products and baked goods are mixed, whipped, pasteurized, frozen, baked, boxed, and bottled for overnight shipment throughout the state. Plant City's *Tour Eiffel* is the Publix water tower, which has candles and is gaily painted to look like a giant birthday cake. (The tower is actually in Polk County while Plant City is in Hillsborough County, but Plant City needs a landmark more than Lakeland does, and it *looks* like it's in Plant City, so I've assigned it to Plant City.)

If you ask any of the Reds about this, of course, you will be rewarded with a blank stare. Plant City's east side is *terra incognita* to the players, who have resisted efforts to lure them out of Tampa's condominiums and into more pastoral digs. This is by way of warning to those fans who hope to catch a glimpse of Eric Davis or Chris Sabo promenading on Plant City's main drag of an evening. Berry unlikely.

Ticket Information: At press time, the Reds had not yet released their 1991 ticket prices. Last year's prices were box $6; reserved $5; bleachers $4. Season-ticket package $84. No phone or credit card orders. For ticket information, write Cincinnati Reds, P.O. Box 2275, Plant City, FL 34289.

Autographs: "The Reds are one of the teams that has become very callous," says Tom Bun-

evich, owner of Bay Area Sports Collectibles in Tampa. "They've got a lot of stars that don't sign. The new stadium is pretty easy, though. They generally don't chase anybody out until after eight o'clock, when the guard comes on."

Hotels: The team hotel is the Holiday Inn Plant City, Exit 13 at I-4, P.O. Box 1102, Plant City, FL 33566; (813) 752-3141. Many veteran players continue to live at condos and golf resorts in the Tampa area. *Cincinnati Post* writer Jerry Crasnick, who normally would join his sports-writing colleagues at the Sailport, a condo in Tampa, beat the traffic last spring by bunking ten minutes the other direction in Lakeland.

Area Attractions

• The annual **Florida Strawberry Festival** and **Hillsborough County Fair.** February 28–March 10. Last year's headliners included Loretta Lynn, Jerry Clower and Brenda Lee, Ricky Skaggs, Tanya Tucker, Charlie Daniels, Waylon Jennings, and Bobby Vinton. Slightly smaller crowds gathered for the Strawberry Shortcake Eating Contest, the Youth Swine Show, and the Best-Decorated Baby Diaper Contest. Hours are from 10:00 A.M. to 10:30 P.M. daily; midway open until midnight. Gate admission is $4, children ten and under free with adult. Stadium shows: reserved seats $7, remaining 13,700 "first come–first served" seats free. For information, call

> "A word about Florida. It's as flat as a barbershop quartet after midnight. It's surrounded by salt water and covered by fresh air. It's a great place if you're a mosquito. An *old* mosquito."
>
> —Jim Murray

RIJO
27

(813) 752-9194. Number for tickets after December 3: (813) 754-1996.

Restaurants, Lounges, and Dives: Asked to recommend something good to eat in Plant City, Kansas City Royals manager John Wathan said, "the sandwiches on the bus." He was joking, of course. For great farm food, the Reds head for the Branch Ranch, a barn of a place on Thonotosassa Road, a little north of I-4. (This has long been a Detroit Tigers hangout; see Ernie Harwell's comments, p. 77.)

"There's a restaurant and lounge at the Holiday Inn," says *Cincinnati Post* baseball writer Jerry Crasnick. "It's decent. And they do have a Burger King. That's probably the best you can do in Plant City. It's pretty dead."

Chamber of Commerce: 303 N. Warnell St., Plant City, FL 33566; (813) 754-3707.

Spring Training Sites: 1895, Mobile, AL; 1896–97, New Orleans; 1898, Fort Worth, TX; 1899, Columbus, GA; 1900, New Orleans; 1901–02, Cincinnati, OH; 1903, Augusta, GA; 1904, Dallas; 1905, Jacksonville, FL; 1906, San Antonio, TX; 1907, Marlin, TX; 1908, St. Augustine, FL; 1909, Atlanta; 1910–11, Hot Springs, AR; 1912, Columbus, GA; 1913, Mobile, AL; 1914–15, Alexandria, LA; 1916–17, Shreveport, LA; 1918, Montgomery, AL; 1919, Waxahachie, TX; 1920, Miami; 1921, Cisco, TX; 1922, Mineral Wells, TX; 1923–30, Orlando; 1931–35, Tampa, FL; 1936, San Juan, PR and Tampa; 1937–42, Tampa; 1943–45, Bloomington, IN; 1946–87, Tampa; 1988–present, Plant City.

Won–Lost Record/Attendance:

Year	Record	Attendance
1989	16–14–2	72,561
1988	16–12–2	79,335
1987	16–9	48,488
1986	16–13	68,881
1985	14–12	47,855

A BACHELOR'S GUIDE TO NIGHTLIFE IN PLANT CITY

(The following businesses are still open at 10:00 P.M.)

- Holiday Inn (lounge)
- Denny's
- Little Caesar's (pizza)
- Popeye's
- The Farm Store (convenience store)
- Buddy Freddy's Restaurant
- Presto (convenience store)
- Hungry Howie's
- Texaco (convenience store)
- Shell Oil (twenty-four hour service station at I-4, Exit 13)
- Sparky's (drive-through chicken and hamburgers)
- Domino's Pizza

WELCOME
TO
DUNEDIN
SISTER CITY TO STIRLING, SCOTLAND

STADIUM INFORMATION

Grant Field
373 Douglas Ave.
Dunedin, FL 34698
(813) 733-9302

How long at present location: Fourteen years
Capacity: 6,000
Dimensions: 335 feet left; 380 feet left-center; 400 feet to center; 365 feet to right-center, 315 feet right.
Directions: From U.S. 19, take State Road 580 to Douglas Ave.; south on Douglas. Ballpark is on southeast corner of Douglas and Beltrees. From Alternate U.S. 19 (the coast highway) in Dunedin, take Main Street east to Douglas, turn right. Ballpark is on left at first light.
Parking: Limited paved and gravel parking at stadium. Additional pay spaces at adjoining supermarket lot.
Training site (until first game): Cecil P. Englebert Complex, 1700 Solon Ave., Dunedin.
Directions to training site: From U.S. 19, go west on State Road 580 to County Road; north on County Road 70 to Solon Avenue; west on Solon to complex, about half a mile.

It's not enough to say that Grant Field was small. It was wonderfully small. It was *little.* You could invite all the fans back to the hotel for drinks and not have to send out for more ice. The grandstand behind home plate was just a few rows deep and covered by a wood roof, and watching a Blue Jays game was a little like watching your kids play.

The scale of the park seemed to affect the players, too. One day two springs ago, when the home plate umpire called the game's first pitch a strike, catcher Ernie Witt turned and shook his hand.

All that has changed. Grant Field was expanded to seat 6,000, so it no longer looks like a high school park. (Although it will still be home to the Dunedin High School Falcons.) The parking lot will be even more hopelessly crowded. Ernie Witt won't shake the umpire's hand.

There is a new press box, too. Before, the press area consisted of a few open boxes painted blue, which was both a blessing and a bother for the media. Seating for the Dunedin-Toronto Blue Jays Booster Club surrounded the press box, and the Boosters tend to be both old and vocal. One spring, *Dallas Morning News* writer Tracy Ringolsby, trying to write his "notes" column while a white-haired booster yelled and hooted a few seats away, finally muttered, "Oh, go have a heart attack!"

Because of limited capacity, tickets for Grant Field were hard to come by. Fortunately, the Phillies' Jack Russell Stadium is just a five-minute drive away, so it was no trick at all to watch the Blue Jays work out in the morning and then catch the Phillies game in the afternoon. Now, with more seats, fans can watch the Phillies practice in the morning and see the Jays play in the afternoon. In fact, the baseball purist could do worse than to rent a cottage somewhere between the two stadiums. The two ballparks together comprise one of the most charming corners of Florida spring baseball.

At least they did. We'll reserve judgment on the "bigger and better" Grant Field.

Ticket Information: All tickets $5 (1990 prices). Stadium ticket office open Monday through Saturday, 10:00 A.M. to 3:00 P.M. in season. After December 1, 1989, write to Blue Jays Spring Training Tickets, P.O. Box 957, Dunedin, FL 34697 or call (813) 733-9302. There is a two-dollar handling charge per order. No phone or credit card orders.

Autograph Opportunities: "In Dunedin, the best times are early in the morning," says card collector Rob Nolan, co-owner of Abner Doubleday Baseball Cards in Dunedin. "Maybe 10 A.M. or 11 A.M., when the players are just getting on the field. If a couple of hundred people are yelling, 'George BELL! George BELL!' no one will sign, but when it's early they feel a little more obligated. The best place is in back of the stands behind the third-base dugout, where the players come out of the dressing room before the game. Most of the Jays are pretty good."

"Their outfielders are notoriously moody," says Bruce Allen, owner of Allen's Baseball Cards of Dunedin. "But Fred McGriff is sensational, real patient with the kids."

"McGriff's just a great guy, he always finds some time to sign," agrees Nolan. "That's a vanishing breed. George Bell? Eight out of ten days he won't sign, but the other two he'll have a smile on his face and come right over and sign."

Hotels: The team hotel is the Ramada Inn Countryside, 2560 U.S. 19 North, Clearwater, FL 34621; (813) 796-1234. Nearby, also on U.S. 19, is the Innisbrook golf and tennis resort—three golf courses, five swimming pools, three dining rooms, and more than a thousand fairway suites, the whole shebang surrounded by a thousand wooded acres alive with ducks and peacocks.

There are numerous small beachfront motels off Alternate U.S. 19 on Clearwater Bay, but most of the players rent condominiums on Clearwater Beach or one of the other Holiday Isles. "In Dunedin," says former Jays slugger and coach John Mayberry, "the veteran players take care of the young guys. The rookies, if they're on the roster, stay at the Ramada for a couple of days and then move in with one of the old guys."

> "Baseball teams go south to cripple their players. In the old days they only stayed a couple of weeks, and they couldn't get many of them hurt in that time, but nowadays they stay till they get them all hurt."
>
> —Will Rogers

Area Attractions

• **Highland Games.** Dunedin's Scots celebrate their heritage every spring with bagpipe competitions, concerts, and traditional contests like the caber toss (a telephone-pole-throwing competition). April 13–20.

• Golf at the **Dunedin Country Club**, 1050 Palm Boulevard. For information and tee times, call (813) 733-2134.

Restaurants, Lounges, and Dives: According to John Mayberry, all the best places have gone out of business. "The L&N Restaurant, across the street from the Ramada, was a great seafood place, but they must have moved it or closed it down. Another place was Prince's, a real good family barbecue. I really miss that. Of course, for barbecue there's always Sonny's."

Among the places most often mentioned by the Jays and the Phillies are a couple of chains on U.S. 19, Chili's and TGI Friday's, and Molly Goodhead's, a popular raw bar that serves up clams, shrimp, grouper, and alligator tail. "I would put in Crabby Bill's in Redington Beach," says card-shop owner Rob Nolan. "It's kind of a rowdy atmosphere, but the food's just dynamite and it's really big with locals, especially the beach crowd. They have their own fishing boats that go out daily, so the food's really fresh. I used to bartend on the beach, so I know."

"Dunedin is pretty limited," says *Toronto Star* baseball writer Neil MacCarl, "but there are a couple of outstanding spots. One is the Bon Appetit at the Jamaica Inn at the foot of Main Street. It's big and on the water, and if you get there early you might catch a nice sunset. The other is called Sabals, and it's also on Main Street. It's small, but it's outstanding. Three young guys started the place a few years ago. They'll have pork tenderloin, chicken, lamb, a couple of shrimp dishes—six or eight things, and the menu changes monthly. It's (team vice president) Pat Gillick's favorite place. There's also Jesse's Dockside on the road to Dunedin Beach. It's very big, very busy and very good. But Jesse's doesn't take reservations. Get there before six, or forget it."

Chamber of Commerce: 434 Main St., Dunedin, FL 33528; (813) 733-3197.

Spring Training Sites: 1976–present, Dunedin.

Won–Lost Record/Attendance:

Year	Record	Attendance
1989	21–10	54,270
1988	18–10–2	42,673
1987	9–11	35,101
1986	15–12	43,263
1985	19–9–1	39,523

STADIUM INFORMATION

Jack Russell Stadium
800 Phillies Drive
Clearwater, FL 34615
(813) 442-8496

How long at present location: Forty-five years
Capacity: 7,000
Dimensions: 340 feet down lines, 400 feet to center
Directions: Route 60 West to Greenwood Street, turn right to Seminole Street, turn right again.
Parking: Grass.
Training site (first two weeks of spring training): Carpenter Field, 615 Old Coachman Road, Clearwater.
Directions to training site: Take U.S. 19 to Drew Street, turn west; make first right onto Old Coachman Road. Carpenter Field is straight ahead.

Clearwater is just right.

That occurred to me about an hour before the Phillies played the Cardinals one day two springs ago, while I was nosing around Jack Russell Stadium looking for something to bitch about. I couldn't find fault with the puffball clouds dotting the blue sky, or the warm sun, or the breeze. There was nothing to dislike about the beautifully cared for old ballpark or the good, green grass. The concessionaires all seemed jovial, the vendors were smiling, organist Wilbur Snapp had the pensioners' toes tapping . . . and the Phillies, too, seemed exuberant, horsing around and laughing as they took their cuts and shagged balls.

I mentioned this to a young reporter in the press room, and he pointed out that the Phillies were no longer pennant contenders. "When Rose and Bowa and those guys were here, it was like the regular season started with the first exhibition game. There was pressure from day one. This Phillies team is younger, and realistically they don't figure to be a World Series team, so the writers and everybody lighten up a bit and enjoy themselves. There's not as much news, but I kind of like it that way. I pretend that it's the 1950s and I'm watching the old players like Richie Ashburn and Robin Roberts. It's like I've got my own Wayback Machine."

The idea of the Wayback Machine appealed to me, because I realize that a link to my own childhood is what I look for in every Florida ballpark. Of all the spring-training towns, Clearwater—with its tidy streets and little stucco houses—most resembles West Palm Beach in the 1950s, and Jack Russell Stadium is the closest to West Palm's old Connie Mack Stadium, where I hung out as a child. In Clearwater, I half expected to see Warren Spahn take the mound against Bobby Shantz, and if they had I would have stayed the whole nine innings.

You may find your baseball Brigadoon in Bradenton or Tucson, but mine is in Clearwater.

Ticket Information: box $7; grandstand $6; all seats reserved. Tickets may be purchased by writing to Philadelphia Phillies Tickets, P.O. Box 10336, Clearwater, FL 34617. No phone orders.

Autograph Opportunities: "When you're talking Clearwater, the best time for autographs is February, not March," says Rob Nolan, co-owner of Abner Doubleday Baseball Cards in Dunedin. "Catch the Phillies at the Carpenter Complex. A couple of years ago at Carpenter, you could walk right up, lean against the batting cages and watch. Now they're roping everything off and it's become a more difficult place, but you can still get guys as they leave the dressing room. Nick Leyva put in a rule that players can't sign till practice is over, so only a few guys will sign now if they think the manager is watching."

"Von Hayes was good this year," says Bruce Allen of Allen's Baseball Cards. "Ricky Jordan was excellent, too. The teams that come in to play at Jack Russell or Grant Field can be accessible also."

"Dale Murphy's always been A-number-one with all the fans," says Scott Winslow, owner of World Baseball Cards in Lake Worth, Florida. "He's gotten a little tired of it, but as superstars go, he's as good as anybody." ("Dale Murphy," echoes collector Bob McMaklin, "will stop and sign for kids if it takes him forty-five minutes.")

Hotels: There is no team hotel. There are many reasonably priced motels, mostly chains, on Highway 19, but the rooms with a view are across the Garden Memorial Causeway on Clearwater Beach. The three bigshot hotels are the Sheraton Sand Key Resort, the Adam's Mark/ Caribbean Gulf Resort Hotel, and the Holiday Inn Clearwater Beach Surfside, but reasonably priced motels and apartments are available up and down Gulf Boulevard.

Area Attractions

- **Gulf beaches.** Clearwater Beach is the most obvious, but the Holiday Isles consist of twenty-eight miles of soft sand beaches. Take the Highway 60 causeway over Clearwater Bay and explore the shore as far south as Treasure Island.
- **Saltwater fishing.** Full- and half-day expeditions, bait and tackle included, embark daily from Clearwater Marina, (813) 446-7666, and Passport Marina in Madeira Beach, (813) 393-1947.
- **Pier fishing.** Fees are modest and several piers are open twenty-four hours. Among the local favorites are Piers 1 and 2 at Fort Desoto, Big Pier 60 at Clearwater Beach, Big Indian Rocks Pier, and the Redington Long Pier on Redington Beach.

Restaurants, Lounges, and Dives: "I guess the secret place that everybody likes is a real small Italian place called Sole de Mare," says Ray Finocchiaro of the *Wilmington News-Journal.* "It's on Gulf Boulevard in the Indian Rocks area. You need reservations and it's only open a few times a week, but the food's great. Bill Giles, the players, the whole Phillies company is seen there a lot."

John Timberlake, general manager of the Clearwater Phillies, recommends Tio Pepe's, a "Spanish" restaurant on Route 60. (Tio Pepe's is also a favorite of Detroit Tigers broadcaster Ernie Harwell.) "Another one that's real popular with the players is Lenny's in Clearwater," says Mashek. "Their specialty is breakfast, particularly omelets." (Also potato knishes, matzo brei, and blintzes "just like Lenny's mother made," according to the ads.)

"The minor-leaguers, all the writers eat at Lenny's," says Finocchiaro. "It's real inexpensive. If you order eggs, you get three flapjacks on the side, a little basket of Danish, and it'll cost you, like three-fifty. It's right by the Carpenter Complex."

Rick Hummel of the *St. Louis Post-Dispatch* throws in a mention for Frenchy's Shrimp and Oyster Cafe in Clearwater, a place noted for both food and spirits. "The Phillies told me about it," he says. "It's a real nice saloon."

Chamber of Commerce: Greater Clearwater, 128 North Osceola Ave., Clearwater, FL 34615; (813) 461-0011.

Spring Training Sites: 1901, Philadelphia; 1902, Washington, D.C.; 1903, Richmond, VA; 1904, Savannah, GA; 1905, Augusta, GA; 1906–08, Savannah, GA; 1909–10, Southern Pines, NC; 1911, Birmingham, AL; 1912, Hot Springs, AR; 1913, Southern Pines, NC; 1914, Wilmington, NC; 1915–18, St. Petersburg, FL; 1919, Charlotte, NC; 1920, Birmingham, AL; 1921, Gainesville, FL; 1922–24, Leesburg, FL; 1925–27, Bradenton, FL; 1928–37, Winter Haven, FL; 1938, Biloxi, MS; 1939, New Braunfels, TX; 1940–42, Miami Beach; 1943, Hershey, PA; 1944–45, Wilmington, DE; 1946, Miami Beach; 1947–present, Clearwater.

Won-Lost Record/Attendance:

Year	Record	Attendance
1989	12–16–2	68,215
1988	13–17–1	64,600
1987	13–11	45,794
1986	16–10	48,367
1985	14–10	46,482

A Whiz Kid Remembers 'Papa'

Dick Sisler, the venerable Cardinals organization batting coach, hit .276 over eight major-league seasons and managed the Cincinnati Reds in the 1960s, but he held baseball's center stage just once—during the 1950 National League pennant race, when he delivered key hit after key hit for the Philadelphia Whiz Kids. On the last day of the season, Sisler jolted Brooklyn Dodgers pitcher Don Newcombe with a tenth-inning, three-run homer at Ebbets Field, giving the Phillies the pennant. So excited by his historic clout was Sisler that day that manager Eddie Sawyer yanked him for the last half-inning in favor of a calmer outfielder. For years afterward, whenever Sisler signed autographs or made personal appearances, fans would mention that home run.

"It's a good thing I hit that one," Sisler says, chuckling over a cigarette, "or maybe I wouldn't be remembered at all."

There he is wrong, for Sisler, in a small way, is a literary immortal. If this were a movie, the camera would follow the twists of smoke rising from Sisler's cigarette, and the frame would brighten and explode into a searing tropical sun: "HAVANA, CUBA—DECEMBER, 1945."

As Sisler tells the story, he was twenty-five years old and just out of the Navy when he reported to play winter ball for the Havana team of the Cuban League. It was the pre-revolution Cuba of strongman Fulgencio Batista—a seamy paradise of palm trees, resort hotels, and glittery gambling casinos. In his first game, Sisler hit two home runs, and the Havana fans roared. In another game, he blasted three home runs off Sal Maglie to become an instant national hero. Gifts poured in. When one of Sisler's shot's cleared the Tropical Stadium wall and landed on the grounds of a brewery, the brewery owner rewarded him with a gold watch. Sisler admits, "I became sort of an idol down there."

Idols get asked out. One night, Sisler was guest of honor at a party on the outskirts of Havana. The host? Ernest Hemingway.

"He was a rough and tough guy," Sisler says. "He stopped what he was doing and came over to talk to me. He was half-loaded, and he said, 'You're a big ballplayer, how about trading punches with me? You hit me first, and then I hit you.'

"I said, 'Mr. Hemingway, I can't take a chance

that I would hurt my hand and not be able to play baseball.' He said he understood."

Not much, as anecdotes go. Sisler left Cuba that spring and never returned. But then, in 1952, Charles Scribner's Sons published a new Hemingway novel called *The Old Man and the Sea.* The book contained this passage:

> "Tell me about the baseball," the boy asked him.
>
> "In the American League it is the Yankees as I said," the old man said happily.
>
> "They lost today," the boy told him.
>
> "That means nothing. The great DiMaggio is himself again."
>
> "They have other men on the team."
>
> "Naturally. But he makes the difference. In the other league between Brooklyn and Philadelphia I must take Brooklyn. But then I think of Dick Sisler and those great drives in the old park. There was nothing ever like him. He hits the longest ball I have ever seen."
>
> "Do you remember when he used to come to the Terrace? I wanted to take him fishing, but I was too timid to ask him. Then I asked you to ask him and you were too timid."
>
> "I know. It was a great mistake. He might have gone with us. Then we would have that for all our lives."

Some years back, Sisler's copy of *The Old Man and the Sea* was stolen from his house in La Jolla, California. The book was a gift from Hemingway. "I hated to lose that book," Sisler says. "He autographed it to me personally,"

Fade to black.

An Interview with Wilbur Snapp, Organist at Jack Russell Stadium

Q: Are you spring baseball's only organist?
A: I think so. Al Lang Stadium in St. Petersburg used to have a live organist, but no more. In fact, when I first came down here from Ohio, I went to the Cardinals to see if they wanted me. They said, "You're welcome to play, but we can't pay you anything for it." Well, I couldn't lug a $10,000 organ to the ballpark for nothing, so I had to look somewhere else. I went to the Phillies and they were interested, but they didn't know if I could play a note. So I said, "I'll bring my organ to the ballpark and play a game for free, and you can decide." Well, I played one song, and they hired me.

Q: What was the song?
A: I don't remember. Probably "Take Me Out to the Ball Game." Anyway, I've played seven seasons for the Phillies now, and in the summer I play for the Clearwater Phillies.

You remember the story about me and the "Three Blind Mice" deal, don't you? That was in the summer Florida State League. One night, the ump at first base missed one a mile, it wasn't even close, and I played "Three Blind Mice." So he ejected me! June 26, 1985—I'll never forget that date. As far as I know, I'm the only organist who ever got thrown out of a game. It was on "Today," "Good Morning America," Paul Harvey had it, *National Geographic* . . . there was even a Japanese newspaper that did a story on it. Yeah, I'm the guy.

Q: What's the penalty for being an outlaw organist?
A: I was fined a hundred dollars by the league, but they waived the fine if I promised not to do it again. And I haven't. I still play "Three Blind Mice," but I do it just before the umpires walk

Ballpark organist Wilbur Snapp

out, not during the game. If a call that bad comes up again, I plan to play "Turkey in the Straw"—because the umpire's a turkey, right?—but I've never had the occasion since.

In my entertainment—I have a band and play programs and dances for mobile home parks, things like that—I make animal balloons. The night I played "Three Blind Mice," the umpires threw me out of the game, but they didn't throw me out of the stadium. So I spent the rest of the evening going around the stands and making balloon mice for people. I think the umpires wished they hadn't thrown me out.

Q: How did you get into playing ballpark organ?

A: I'm a retired music dealer from Ohio. For seventeen years I had a keyboard store right across from the ballpark in Springfield, Ohio, and I used to play for the Stroh's Invitational Tournament every year. That was a slow-pitch softball tournament. Teams would come in from all over the United States. We'd just take the organ right across the street, and that's how I got started. I got to know all these big-league organists because I was in the organ business. Eddie Layton, the Yankees organist, I knew him. Shay Torrent, who played for the California Angels. You know, I didn't realize how little they paid big-league organists. I was surprised to find out that the Angels organist only got $125 a game.

Q: What kind of music do spring-training audiences want to hear?
A: We have basically a retired audience. They like the music of the thirties, the fifties, the sixties . . . which is good, because that's all I know. I have a repertoire of two or three thousand songs, but I'm an untrained musician. I never had any lessons, I don't read any music, I'm self-taught. I just remember all these songs. When Pete Rose used to come here as a player, I'd play "Ramblin' Rose" when he came to the plate. For Ron Darling of the Mets, I'd play "Darling Clementine." When a pitcher gets taken out, I play "There'll Be Some Changes Made." And if we get way behind, it's "I Never Felt More Like Singing the Blues." One time, Sparky Anderson and an umpire got into a chin-to-chin at first base, so I put a real sweet setting on the organ and played "I Love You Truly." That kind of broke up the argument.

Of course, I play requests like "Happy Birthday," and I try to get the crowd going by playing something with a beat. It adds to the game. The organ I have is a fantastic piece of merchandise, too. It hooks into the P.A., and the sound at Jack Russell Stadium is actually better than at many of the big-league parks.

Q: You sound pretty busy for somebody who's retired.
A: It's not really work. When I get up in the morning, I don't think, "Oh, I've got to go to the ballpark." I think, "Oh, I *get* to go to the ballpark." My wife sells programs, we meet a nice bunch of people, we get to know the players well. Did you see the table downstairs, the ball bats made into hat racks? I do that, too. I've made hundreds of them. I started woodcraft after I retired, and my wife and I would take the toys and stuff I made and go to craft shows. Now I collect the broken bats from several major-league camps and make them into hat racks and pen sets. I also make a little toy car out of the end of the bat. I call it the "batmobile." I can hardly keep up with the demand. You know, most people's hobbies cost money, but mine make money.

I've got to say, also, that the Phillies take care of me, they're a tremendous organization. They pay me fairly . . . and the tip jar is good!

Q: Any thoughts about coming out of retirement?
A: No, not really. I've had other parks after me to play organ, but I'll be sixty-nine before long and I'm not interested in making long trips. No, retirement's the best job I've ever had.

STADIUM INFORMATION

Al Lang Stadium
180 Second Ave. S.E.
St. Petersburg, FL 33701
(813) 896-4641

How long at present location: Forty-seven years
Capacity: 7,004
Dimensions: 330 feet down lines, 410 feet to center
Directions: I-275 to Exit 9; follow signs to park.
Training site: The Cardinals minor-league facility, Busch Complex, 7901 30th Ave. N., St. Petersburg, FL; (813) 345-5300.
Directions to training site: From Tampa, cross bridge and travel south on I-275 to 22nd Ave. North; follow 22nd Ave. N. to 80th St., turn right. Complex is a quarter of a mile ahead on right.
Parking at Al Lang: Paved parking. Meter parking on surrounding streets. The lot at the Hilton, across the street, is for hotel guests only; guards are posted.

"Candy apples! Watermelons! Ice cold hot dogs!"

The vendor's cry takes a moment to sink in. Foreheads furrow; heads cock quizzically.

"Don't be a meanie, buy a weenie!"

You see people turning to ask, "What'd he say?"

That's the effect Tommy Walton has on first-time visitors to Al Lang Stadium. The Cardinals are supposedly the resident artists, but Walton, better known as "The Singing Hot Dog Vendor," usually steals the show. While Joe Torre's boys are busy trying to steal first base, Walton roams the stands with *a cappella* versions of tunes like, "He's Got the Whole World in His Hands," "East Side, West Side," and "Born in the U.S.A." He's been doing it for fourteen years, and he must live on smiles and applause because he's too busy singing to sell many franks. ("Now how about taking those hands," he pleads after one ovation, "run 'em in your pocket and buy a hot dog?")

Walton's got a strong, rich voice and great stage presence—the lettering on his apron declares him to be "World's Greatest Singing Vendor"—but his way with lyrics takes some getting used to. His version of "America the Beautiful" contains eyebrow-raisers like "purple mountain's modesty" and "mourn our good with brotherhood." But heck, Walton's no lounge lizard playing from a fake book; he's the genuine grandstand Pavarotti singing from the heart.

I dwell on Walton because it's the sideshow that makes Al Lang so much fun. The stadium itself has all the charm of a bridge abutment, but downtown St. Petersburg, with its yacht basin and high-rise buildings, is one of the Grapefruit League's prettiest settings. And it's the only Florida park (with the possible exception of West Palm Beach, which borders a mall), where it's practical to park your car and walk to a restaurant or department store.

But please, don't eat a heavy lunch. Save room for a Tommy Walton hot dog.

Ticket Information: At press time, the Cardinals had not yet released their 1991 ticket information. For ticket information, call the Cardinals customer service line, (314) 421-3060.

Autograph Opportunities: "A lot of St. Louis players are tough autographs," says Dunedin collector Rob Nolan, "so it can be difficult at Al Lang. Ozzie Smith *used* to be good."

The Cardinals clubhouse door is under the first-base grandstand, behind a guarded gate, but players sometimes sign when they come out this door or one of the other stadium exits to get their cars. Autographs are easier across town at the Busch Complex, where players sign over a low cyclone fence near the clubhouse. "McGee, Coleman, and Ozzie Smith often come together," says Tom Bunevich. "They'll hop out of a mini-van and it's like a hundred-yard dash straight to the door."

Hotels: The team hotel is the St. Petersburg Hilton and Towers, 333 First St. South, St. Petersburg, FL 33701; (813) 894-5000. The Hilton is convenient to the stadium (right across the street), but not so convenient to the training site, which is miles across town.

"I think the most memorable place I have ever stayed is the Don CeSar Hotel in St. Petersburg Beach," says baseball writer and author Tom Boswell. "It's mammoth, it's Pepto-Bismol pink, it's like something out of Walt Disney's *Fan-*

tasia. It ought to be in bad taste, but it's wonderful, which just proves that the only good excess is wretched excess. And it's got a good beach. They say that Ring Lardner and the like stayed there fifty or sixty years ago, which I hope is true because I want to believe it. I would say if you want to bust your budget just one place, stay at the Don CeSar for a couple of days. It'll be $500 for the weekend instead of $200, but it's worth it."

> "Indeed, on a spring-training field, almost everything seems promising. It is relaxed and wisecracky, an atmosphere in which it's hard to wrap the mind around specters and curses. Maybe it is only a rehearsal for real life, which can get nasty."
>
> —Sydney H. Schanberg

Area Attractions

• The **Don CeSar Hotel** . . . and not just because you'll see Tom Boswell or *Sports Illustrated*'s Steve Wulf looking suave in the lobby. It's on the National Register of Historic Places. Babe Ruth and Lou Gehrig stayed here, Clarence Darrow and F. Scott Fitzgerald (and Zelda) descended its grand staircase. You should, too. 3400 Gulf Blvd., St. Petersburg Beach.
• Greyhound racing at **Derby Lane,** 10490 Gandy Blvd. (813) 576-1361. Open daily except Sunday from 7:00 P.M.

Restaurants, Lounges, and Dives: *SI*'s Steve Wulf, a longtime fan of the Hurricane Lounge on Pass-a-Grille Beach, returned last year with woeful tidings: "It's totally ruined. The food is still good, but the lines are long and the waitresses are surly." Rick Hummel of the *St. Louis Post-Dispatch* says that the Hurricane is still one of the in spots, but he agrees with Wulf that the crowds are daunting. "It's like Yogi Berra said—nobody goes there, it's too crowded. The place I go to a couple of times a year is Bern's Steak House in Tampa. You've got to call a couple of days ahead to get a reservation, but it's wonderful steak and you get to pick the size and kind you want."

Marty Noble of *Newsday* likes Bern's so much that he once drove there from the winter meetings in Ft. Lauderdale, a round trip of 480 miles. "It's the best restaurant in the world," he says. "Everything is absolutely exquisite. The wine list is a like a phone directory. They grow their own vegetables across the steet. It's a *value*. You can drop fifty bucks there and it's worth it. I've never had a single meal anywhere else as good as what I get at Bern's every time." He adds: "Brazilian Snow is what a lot of guys have for dessert, but I have the raspberry sherbet."

"The players pretty much stick to their condos and their families and maybe only go out for a beer," says Hummel, "but I do see a lot of them at the dog track, Derby Lane. The Derby Club is the name of the restaurant there, and they specialize in steak and fish, prime rib, grouper. I spend more time there than anyplace else. It's not inexpensive, but if you can afford to go to the track in the first place, you can probably afford to eat there."

Wulf's new recommendation, subject to change without notice: "P.J.'s at Madeira Beach—very good seafood."

Chamber of Commerce: 6990 Gulf Blvd., St. Petersburg Beach, FL 33706; (813) 360-6957.

Spring Training Sites: 1901–02, St. Louis; 1903, Dallas; 1904, Houston; 1905, Marlin Springs, TX; 1906–08, Houston; 1909–10, Little Rock; 1911, West Baden, IN; 1912, Jackson, MS; 1913, Columbus, GA; 1914, St. Augustine, FL;

COLEMAN
29

1915–17, Hot Wells, TX; 1918, San Antonio, TX; 1919, St. Louis; 1920, Brownsville, TX; 1921–22, Orange, TX; 1923–24, Bradenton, FL; 1925, Stockton, CA; 1926, San Antonio, TX; 1927–29, Avon Park, FL; 1930–36, Bradenton, FL; 1937, Daytona Beach, FL; 1938–42, St. Petersburg; 1943–45, Cairo, IL; 1946–present, St. Petersburg.

Won–Lost Record/Attendance:

Year	Record	Attendance
1989	16–12	78,712
1988	10–18–1	74,981
1987	17–6	61,169
1986	12–15	65,833
1985	8–14	54,318

At the Dali Museum with Quiz . . .

Dan Quisenberry, the recently retired legendary mustachioed submarine pitcher, threw two scoreless innings in relief for the Cardinals one day in St. Petersburg. Afterward, he showered and went with the author to see the collected works of the legendary mustachioed surrealist, Salvador Dali. "It's about time I saw some of his work," said Quisenberry. "I've been dropping his name in conversation for years."

The Salvador Dali Museum and gift shop is on the waterfront in Poynter Park, a short drive from Al Lang Stadium. When Quiz passed through the turnstiles, he went straight to the nearest wall of paintings and let his eyes wander for a few minutes. Then he spoke. (For purposes of confusion, the Q below stands for Quisenberry, the A for Author.)

QUIZ: My first impression is that he paints a lot of naked, cold women. My second impression is that he looks like a relief pitcher himself. And after seeing a few of these weirder pictures, I wonder if he would have gotten past the '83 drug investigation.
AUTHOR: This one is called *Paranoia,* 1935–36. Are those knights jousting on top of the torso?

Q: Either that or the horse got stabbed in the rump, I'm not sure.
A: This is called *Puzzle of Autumn*.

Q: I'd be puzzled if autumn looked like that, too.
A: There seem to be some topless ladies in tutus.

Q: More naked cold women. Looks like Spain.
A: Have you been to Spain?

Q: No, but I saw a picture of it once. Look, on the back of that car . . . that looks like America. There's Florida, further east . . . And now we have a ballet dancer, who looks somewhat depressed, with another relief pitcher.
A: *Three Young Surrealist Women*.

Q: Once again, more naked cold women.
A: This has some of the classic Dali business. Observe the melting cello.

Q: Wow!
A: You said "Wow." Is it the heads?

Q: Yeah, the heads are . . . flowered heads. Reminds me of early Jefferson Airplane lyrics.
A: *Sentimental Colloquy*? I like the waterfall coming out of the piano lid.

Q: Me, too.
A: . . . and now we have a lot of cadaverous-looking characters on bicycles with boulders on their heads and trailing veils, and with perspective lines receding like a superhighway in the distance.

Q: And a thumbprint or something. I think we have to remember the world was at war during this picture.

A: *Daddy Longlegs of the Evening. Hope!*, 1940. Here, a whole human form has that melting quality. She's stretched or puddled over a branch . . . another melted cello, another horse coming out of the cannon.

Q: I don't see the hope in it.
A: *Old Age, Adolescence, Infancy.* More faces.

Q: Fenway Park with holes in the wall.
A: This reminds me of that optical trick, the image of two vases which is simultaneously two faces in profile.

Q: Yeah. Look at this nose. I just realized that this is an older woman and a young boy. These eyes are really little buildings off in the distance.
A: Do you have any art at home?

Q: Yeah, I have some prints. Not of Dali. I couldn't even tell you who I have. Watercolors. They're more to go with the wallpaper than anything else.
A: People might expect you to have art that makes a bold statement of some kind.

Q: Well, we have a Williamsburg house. Or rather we have a new house that is pretending to be of that era, so we tried to get art that looks like that era. Dali wouldn't fit.
A: Here's a nice one. *Slave Market with the Disappearing Bust of Voltaire.*

Q: Okay. This must be the bust of Voltaire . . . with no Voltaire, huh? I'm lost.
A: Maybe if you step back . . .

Q: That might help. Because over here, if you step back, you see the faces more than the wall . . . No, I'm still lost. Shall we look at some of the big works?
A: By all means.

Q: *The Discovery of America by Christopher Columbus*, 1958-59. Very religious imagery.
A: I wouldn't have identified this as a Dali. It doesn't have any of his trademark images.

Q: Crosses. Don't those look like lances in the background, too?
A: The crosses at the top are floating horizontally. Does that suggest death? Like coffins. There's no motion implied.

Q: I see these lances and flags in the background like the hordes are coming. And who is this coming out of the banner, Joan of Arc? It makes you want to read the program notes.
A: *Nature Morte et Vivant.* Everything's hanging in the air over the table . . . spilling . . . liquids . . .

Q: It makes me think of Gene Mauch, the manager. He used to knock over the spread whenever they'd get beat.
A: Dali's *in* this one.

Q: Sunday chapel service. There's the Pope in the middle, a Michelangelo God from the Sistine Chapel. 1960. That's close to the time of God being dead in *Time* magazine, isn't it?
A: It was also the time of the Ecumenical Council. Here's *Hallucinogenic Toreador.* Get a load of all the Venus de Milos.

Q: There's Mariana Duncan up in the left corner. And they're in the L.A. Coliseum.
A: There's the bull. Large blue-bottle flies.

Q: A sunbather on a raft in the middle of the pool.
A: Optical dots . . . (VOICE: "The gallery will close in ten minutes.")

Q: (Heading for the door) Did you see the two Dominican shortstops? That was the first thing I noticed when I came in. Here it is. I call it *Two Dominican Shortstops.*
A: Dali called it *Two Gypsy Lads.* 1920-21.

Q: There weren't any Dominican shortstops in those years.
A: Even if there were, those guys would certainly be coaches by now.

Q: Or pinch-hitters. And here's a World Series celebration. The fat ladies are singing.
A: Is that how it felt when the Royals won the World Series in 1985?

Q: Yeah. The locker room didn't look like that, though. If there's time, I'd like to look at the one with the blue light coming out of it. (Crosses room)
A: *Apparatus and Hand.* Has your hand ever felt like that?

Q: Yeah. Playing catch with Tony Pena on a cold day. These are sinker-slider bone chips on the elbow. And this is classic . . . when you see the batter hit the foul ball off his toe? This is what's going on underneath.
A: It's even called *The Batter.*

Q: No, it's *The Bather.*
A: Close enough. The blood vessels, the swelling, the inflammation.

Q: It looks like it aches.
A: Does it strike you as odd that so many of these paintings are about baseball?

Q: (No answer)
A: *Oeufs Sur le Plat sans le Plat.* "Eggs on a plate without the plate."

Q: Why does he do it in French if he's Spanish? Is that "without the plate"—*Sans le Plat?*
A: Yeah. It looks like a broken egg being hung in effigy.

Q: Dali was before his time in nutritional analysis. Over here (moving), this is left-center in old Yankee Stadium before they moved the fences in. Death Valley. (Pause) A bunch of us want to go to the Metropolitan Museum the next time we're in New York. Have you been there?
A: Yes. It's very big. (Approaching exit) Well, would you recommend the Dali Museum to a visitor to Saint Petersburg?

Q: I definitely would. It's the perfect rain-delay killer. You could spend hours in here and not be the worse for it.
A: You liked it.

Q: (Nodding) I'd say Dali was the ultimate knuckleball expressionist.

(The Salvador Dali Museum, 1000 Third St. South, St. Petersburg, FL 33701. Open Tuesday through Saturday, 10:00 A.M. to 5:00 P.M., Sunday, 12 noon to 5 P.M. Closed Mondays.)

GENERAL ADMISSION
AND CHILDREN

STADIUM INFORMATION

McKechnie Field
17th Ave. West and 9th St.
Bradenton, FL 34208
(813) 747-3031

How long at present location: Twenty-three years
Capacity: 5,000
Dimensions: 340 feet down lines, 359 feet to left-center, 410 feet to center, 373 feet to right-center
Directions: From St. Petersburg, cross Skyway Bridge to Route 41 South into Bradenton; at 17th Avenue (do not confuse with 17th St.), make right to ballpark. From I-75, take Route 64 West to 9th St.; turn left to stadium.
Parking: Stadium lot is tiny; spillover is handled by neighborhood lots, mostly dirt and gravel.

Decline and desuetude are the themes in Pirateland. If you liked the Frank Sinatra song, "There Used to Be a Ballpark Here," you'll love McKechnie Field, Bradenton's ode to peeling paint, sagging bleachers, and rust. This is not meant as a knock. McKechnie is spring baseball's haunted house, and—as the movie *Field of Dreams* proved—baseball loves its haunts.

You can carry this sort of thing too far, though. Three years ago, a man was killed here chasing a foul ball into the street. The year before, Hall-of-Fame outfielder Edd Roush collapsed and died in the Pirates press room. ("On opening day this year we renamed it the Edd Roush Press Room," says Pirates public relations director Rick Cerrone. "I kid that we've got the only press room named for a guy who didn't like the press.") The stadium has taken these setbacks hard, and sometimes seems too weary to go on.

The Pirates would put it differently. They say McKechnie Field is no longer "viable," and they have put Bradenton and Manatee County on notice that they want a new facility, something shiny with bright lights, a real parking lot, and a green rug to play on. They will get it, of course—if not from Bradenton, from some other eager suitor—and McKechnie will fall to the wrecker's ball.

The funny thing is, McKechnie Field is not nearly as old as it looks. It was built in 1953.

Must have seen a ghost.

Ticket Information: At press time, the Pirates had not yet released their 1991 ticket prices. Last year's ticket prices were box $6; reserved $5; general admission $4 (children $1). For current prices and information, call (412) 323-5046.

Autograph Opportunities: "I'm from Pittsburgh, I'm a big Pirate fan," confesses Tampa card-shop owner Tom Bunevich. "The best place to get the Pirates is at Pirate City, because there they have to walk from their cars. Four years ago when they were in last place, the players would practically take you out to dinner. This year, you had to work hard."

"You want to get on the right-field side, because that's where they start their drills," says collector Rob Nolan. "Andy Van Slyke is one of

PIRATES
8

the hardest to obtain in the big leagues. He ignores people, just walks right by."

Hotels: The Pirates have no team hotel. Young players and team officials stay at the club's minor-league complex, Pirate City, 1701 Roberto Clemente Memorial Drive (27th St. East), Bradenton, FL 34208. Pirate City is closed to the public. Many players rent slick condominiums on Longboat Key or Anna Maria Island, but fans who want to spend a little less will find modest beach cottages along Bradenton Beach. Part of the price is the heavy traffic and a certain seaside tackiness, but young fans with a taste for beer and bikinis will have a blast. The top-of-the-line beach hotels (Hilton, Holiday Inn, Colony Beach Resort) are on Longboat Key. The best downtown hotel is the Holiday Inn Riverfront.

Area Attractions

- **Legendary Golf.** "One of the great things about Bradenton is they've opened the most incredible miniature golf course," says Pirates public relations director Rick Cerrone. "This is not putting through windmills and apes' feet. This is par-4s where you've got to wrap your shot around water hazards and rocks. It even has sand traps. It's a lot of fun, and lots of players go there." Two eighteen-hole courses. It's at 51st Street West and Cortez Road, behind the power plant.
- Beaches. **Bradenton Beach, Holmes Beach,** and **Anna Maria Beach,** north to south, on Anna Maria Island.
- The **Bishop Planetarium,** 201 10th St. West (U.S. 41), Bradenton. Adults $2, students $1.50. (813) 746-STAR.

Restaurants, Lounges, and Dives: "Probably the most-frequented places are on Anna Maria Island," says Cerrone. "The Sandbar, right on the gulf, has great seafood at good prices. A block away, there's a crowded place called Fast Eddie's—very bustling, everything is giant portions." According to Cerrone, the Pirates also like Chili's, across from the Desoto Mall, and the Olive Garden Italian restaurant on U.S. 41.

Hal McRae, a Bradenton native, is remembered as perhaps the greatest designated hitter in baseball history. He coaches for the Expos now, but he still gets out for an occasional meal. "My favorite is L'Auberge," he says, "a French restaurant out on the end of Longboat Key, near Bradenton Beach. It's a family-owned place. I usually get the fish, the grouper, but their beef is good, too. And for dessert, I really like those crepes."

Chamber of Commerce: 222 10th St. West, Bradenton, FL 34205; (813) 748-3411.

Spring Training Sites: 1900, Thomasville, GA; 1901–14, Hot Springs, AR; 1915–17, Dawson Springs, KY; 1918, Jacksonville, FL; 1919, Birmingham, AL; 1920–23, Hot Springs, AR; 1924–34, Paso Robles, CA; 1935, San Bernardino, CA; 1936, San Antonio, TX; 1937–42, San Bernardino, CA; 1943–45, Muncie, IN; 1946, San Bernardino, CA; 1947, Miami Beach; 1948, Hollywood, CA; 1949–52, San Bernardino, CA; 1953, Havana, Cuba; 1954, Fort Pierce, FL; 1955–68, Fort Myers; 1969–present, Bradenton.

Won-Lost Record/Attendance:

Year	Record	Attendance
1989	16–16	55,526
1988	17–16	58,579
1987	13–13	41,771
1986	16–10	38,475
1985	6–18	39,715

In the Heat of the Day

There are sun people and there are shade people. The creeping shadow of a ballpark roof on a breezeless Florida afternoon is as territorially significant to a baseball fan as a coral reef is to a shark. Until recently, some major-league teams sold spring exhibition tickets in two categories: *shade* reserved seats and *sun* bleachers.

When I was a kid, West Palm Beach was the spring-training headquarters of the Philadelphia-Kansas City Athletics. Old Connie Mack Stadium was just down the hill and across the parking lot from my school, Central Elementary. The exhibition games were only half-over when the school bell rang in the afternoon, and I often bought a ticket or snuck in past the dozing turnstile guard.

A general admission ticket entitled one to a foot or so of gray, splintered plank amid muttering old men cooking in the sun, but I couldn't sit still for more than an inning in their company. I tried to copy their antiquarian squint, shielding my eyes from the sun with a program, but my forearm would burn red in minutes, and sweat would streak my face. To avoid scorching, I squirmed between the planks and braces and dropped to the ground, to the cool shadows beneath the bleachers, to the graveyard of crumpled cups and spilled popcorn. For the rest of the game I exposed myself to the relentless sunlight for scant moments at a time, peering at the ballplayers through chicken-wire barriers until the old men growled at me to move.

Out past first base, down the right-field line and beyond the sun bleachers—beyond a railing, beyond a chicken-wire partition—were still more bleachers. These were called the "colored stands." I don't trust my memory, but it seems to me that these bleachers were always crowded.

Black people walked the few short blocks from "Niggertown," from the corner groceries and rocking-chair rotted porches on Tamarind Avenue. They came from the sandspur and junk-car backyards, from the barbecue dens of weekend violence, from the stucco storefront churches. Many of them were old, with lines like ropes creasing their black faces—bony, wrinkled hands to fascinate and frighten a child. They wore baggy trousers, secondhand cotton shirts, straw hats or baseball caps, and old shoes grown hard and lusterless with age. They entered the ballpark almost unnoticed from a separate entrance, a broken-down gate in the wall behind the right-field bleachers, next to the railroad tracks.

(There were signs stenciled on the outside of the stadium walls, painted arrows with captions: COLORED SPECTATORS ENTRANCE. There were signs on everything in Florida in the 1950s—rest rooms, water fountains, buses. The signs in the buses read: "White Passengers Seat from Front—Colored Passengers Seat from Rear.")

To a white child, the colored bleachers were exotic. And pathetic. And menacing. It was easy to picture those old black folk, with their children and grandchildren huddled about them, as slaves, shackled together in the holds of slave ships.

They were not slaves, of course. They were baseball fans.

"Segregation isn't something any of us were proud of," Steve Boros told me some springs ago, wiping his face with a towel in the clubhouse at Terry Park in Ft. Myers. The Royals first-base coach (later the manager of the A's and Padres) was remembering his first years in professional baseball in the mid-1950s, when the color line had been "broken" by Jackie Robinson and other talented black athletes, but segregation still prevailed.

"It was embarrassing," the former infielder recalled. "It was for me, anyway. I felt sheepish around my black teammates. I remember how shocked I was when I came to spring training for the first time with the Tigers and saw water fountains marked white and colored."

Boros sat on the stool in front of his alcove. "I'd *heard* of it, of course, but I was still shocked. I guess I'd led a sheltered life in Michigan."

Boros's memories of the Sally League, which employed black ballplayers in the late 1950s, were tarnished by numerous examples of crude prejudice. "I still remember a white fan yelling at our pitcher, who was facing a black batter—'Hit that nigger in the head!' And I remember an incident in 1958 with the Augusta, Georgia, club. We had a birthday party for Billy Springfield, a black player who was also going to law school. His landlady threw the party, and there were both white and black couples. Well, someone called the police and the police broke into the party. It was just a birthday party, but some wild rumors got started. And the next thing you know, the team sent all our black players away to other clubs." Boros shook his head. "It's hard to believe, but it happened."

It also happened, routinely, that black ballplayers were denied accommodations on road trips. "In 1960, when I was with Denver and we traveled to Houston, we dropped the black players off at a rooming house outside town." The memory was obviously uncomfortable to Boros. "The rest of us went in and stayed at the Rice Hotel. I can remember just five or six years ago, some club had a big thing about

white boys rooming with black boys. Nobody gives it a thought now. We've come a long way since 1958 or 1960.

"But," he added softly, "we shouldn't have had to.

"The ironic thing is that there were more black fans back then. Now there are more black players—and fewer black fans."

Boros's observation was accurate. Spring-training crowds today are white. The colored bleachers, if they still existed, would be sparsely populated. The migration of blacks north to urban centers is one plausible explanation for the decline in interest. "It's just a feeling I have," Boros said, "but I feel that black fans enjoy basketball and football more than baseball. They seem to like something a little faster-paced." He could remember, however, when the Brooklyn Dodgers commanded intense black loyalty—so intense that out-of-town blacks would pile into cars and drive to Lakeland to pack the stadium when the Tigers played the Dodgers. "The aspirations of black people were such that they could identify with the black players on the Dodgers. Today, black fans seem to identify more with basketball."

Outside on the hot field, Hal McRae leaned against the batting cage while the other Royals took their cuts and shagged flies. McRae echoed Boros's observation that the black baseball fan was a vanishing breed. "You don't see that many black fans any more," he nodded cheerfully. "Most of the old ones have died or are too old to come out, I guess. A lot of those fans were old players from the black leagues. They really loved baseball."

McRae grew up in Bradenton, but, surprisingly, never saw a major-league game as a youngster. As a result, he did not suffer—or witness—the indignities of the colored bleachers. He understood, however, the fall-off of interest in baseball. "The black fans felt closer to the players then," he said. "The players were part of the community. They had to be—they had to have somebody take them in. They socialized together and went to church together and everything."

Rooming houses were a luxury to some black ballplayers, who stayed at strangers' homes on the recommendations of friends and relatives. Hank Aaron, in fact, used to stay up the street from McRae's mother-in-law on Second Street West in Bradenton.

(Today, a black major-leaguer commands a salary that would have stunned the fans in the colored bleachers. He is not likely to be found sharing a bed with a half-brother in East St. Louis or cooking on a hot plate in a cheap rooming house.)

"The housing situation is different," McRae explained. "By law. There are more choices open to blacks. Back then, people took you in and took care of you, and you felt you belonged and were welcome. But now you can live anyplace you can pay the rent and feel the same thing."

The same thing? Well, not exactly. McRae admitted that the old closeness, the sense of community and purpose black fans shared with black athletes, is gone, perhaps forever. "Today you don't find black players going out that much in the community," he said. But there was no sense getting sentimental about a cultural climate that had forced blacks closer together by degrading them. "That's not the ideal situation," he said, "to live in someone's house."

The ideal situation, of course, is to live where you choose, to work at what you choose, to *be* what you choose. The colored bleachers mocked this notion. Any kid with a touch of Huck Finn in him absorbed their meaning sooner or later—recognized the arbitrary nature of justice, the fragility of free will, the elusiveness of empathy. Life was not simply a question of sunny seats versus shady seats, but of more painful choices, and sometimes of no choice at all.

You didn't have to believe in ghosts to know that those bleachers were haunted.

STADIUM INFORMATION

Ed Smith Stadium
2700 12th St.
Sarasota, FL 34237
(813) 954-5722

How long at present location: Two years
Capacity: 7,500
Dimensions: 340 feet down lines, 390-foot alleys, 410 feet to center
Directions: From I-75, take Fruitville Exit, go west to Tuttle and turn right; stadium is on left at Twelfth and Tuttle.
Parking: Large stadium lot, $2.00.

"I went to see the Yankees play the White Sox in Sarasota," says ABC-TV's Dick Schaap, "and I went to the wrong stadium. I went to Payne Park, and I didn't know anything was wrong. I was just surprised it was so easy to find a parking space."

You could argue about who made the mistake, Schaap or the White Sox. "The new stadium is not as nice," he says. "I like Payne Park."

My own notes, after visiting Ed Smith Stadium for the first time, are revealing: "Similar to Port Charlotte, maybe bigger . . . Big roof, lots of blue seats, bleachers down both lines . . . Big capacity, but grandstand not too tall . . . Pretty . . . Grass field . . . Huge wide aisles (for wheelchairs?), easy to walk . . . Very nice . . . Huge dugouts."

The rest of the page is blank.

Somehow, a ballpark ought to leave you with a stronger impression than "lots of blue seats." Maybe this place will take on a patina with time, but for now it looks like a park that memories will have a hard time sticking to.

Still, it's . . . very nice.

Ticket Information: box $7.50; reserved $6; general admission $4 (1990 prices). Spring training tickets for the 1991 season can be ordered after January 1 and are also available at Ticketmaster outlets. Cash or checks accepted. Charge orders are accepted only at Ticketmaster outlets. Write Ed Smith Stadium, 2700 12th St., Sarasota, FL 34237, (813) 954-4101 or Sarasota Sports Committee, P.O. Box 1702, Sarasota, FL 34230, (813) 953-3388.

Autograph Opportunities: "The new park is a lot tougher," says collector Bruce Allen. "It's not as bad as Port St. Lucie or Baseball City, but it's tough." "The White Sox are pretty easy," says Tom Bunevich. "Carlton Fisk is pretty good."

Hotels: The team hotel is the Days Inn, 4900 North Tamiami Trail, Sarasota, FL 34234; (813) 355-9721. The beachfront hotels and condos are on Siesta Key, Lido Key, and Longboat Key. (The Colony Beach and Tennis Resort, the Diplomat Resort, and Beach Castle are all on Longboat Key.) On the mainland, the Hyatt Sarasota is the major hotel, but there are many, many motels along the Tamiami Trail (U.S. 41).

Area Attractions

• John Ringling, the circus impresario, threw up a little house on Sarasota Bay and called it **Ca'**

d'Zan. (The name means "House of John.") As Venetian Gothic palazzos go, this is about as fine as you'll find outside Venice, Italy. The admission price gets you the run of the sixty-eight-acre estate, a tour of Ringling's fabulous art collection, and the famous **Circus Museum.** (5401 Bayshore Drive)

• **Bellm's Cars and Music of Yesterday**, 5500 North Tamiami Trail; (813) 355-6228. Thousands of antique music boxes, calliopes, classic cars, and race cars. Open daily. Adults $5, children six to sixteen $2.25.

• **Sarasota Jungle Gardens**, 3701 Bayshore Road; (813) 355-5305. Flamingoes, parrots, leopards, lots of flowers, and a bird-and-reptile show in a sixteen-acre jungle. Open daily 9:00 A.M. to 5:00 P.M. Adults $5.95, children thirteen and under $2.95; children under two free.

Restaurants, Lounges, and Dives: "The Columbia Restaurant is probably the most famous for dining as well as dancing at night," says Mark Ruda of the *Arlington Heights Daily Herald.* "You see a lot of players there, that's for sure. I think Michelangelo's, an Italian restaurant, would be my favorite. For stone crabs, I'd say Phillippi Creek. It's a very casual, laid-back place, and it has some of the best raw seafood you'll get down there. As far as night life goes, Club Bandstand was the hottest place this year. It's a disco in the Quay Shopping Center on the Inlet—a players' hangout . . . and packed."

"The best stone crabs are at Abbey's Raw Bar," says *Dallas Morning News* baseball writer Tracy Ringolsby.

Chamber of Commerce: 1551 2nd St., Sarasota, FL 34236; (813) 955-8187.

Spring Training Sites: 1901–02, Excelsior Springs, MO; 1903, Mobile, AL; 1904, Marlin Springs, TX; 1905–06, New Orleans; 1907, Mexico City; 1908, Los Angeles; 1909–10, San Francisco; 1911, Mineral Wells, TX; 1912, Waco, TX; 1913–15, Paso Robles, CA; 1916–19, Mineral Wells, TX; 1920, Waco, TX; 1921, Waxahachie, TX; 1922–23, Seguin, TX; 1924, Winter Haven, FL; 1925–28, Shreveport, LA; 1929, Dallas; 1930–32, San Antonio, TX; 1933–42, Pasadena, CA; 1943–44, French Lick, IN; 1945, Terre Haute, IN; 1946–50, Pasadena, CA; 1951, Pasadena/Palm Springs, CA; 1952, Pasadena/El Centro, CA; 1953, El Centro, CA; 1954–59, Tampa; 1960–present, Sarasota.

> "Time was when you could stroll into the park, watch coaches bat fungoes and then take in four or five innings before leaving. Only the most unsophisticated spectator would cheer for his team. Now you see standing ovations for routine plays and actual disappointment when the 'home' team loses. All this for nothing more than a limbering-up exercise."
>
> —Bill Bravick, North Port, Florida, in a letter to *Sports Illustrated*

Won–Lost Record/Attendance:

Year	Record	Attendance
1989	15–23	88,026
1988	13–18	61,078
1987	15–15	54,052
1986	15–15	66,016
1985	19–13–1	60,988

HOOTERS
ARE
WONDERFUL
ON 41
SOMEWHERE NEAR
COLONIAL
5

THE 1990 'BILLBIE' AWARDS

Since a baseball stadium is one of the few environments that is actually enhanced by outdoor advertising, the Society for the Encouragement of Bigger and Better Baseball Billboards (SEBBBB) hands out "Billbies" for the year's best outfield signs. Last year's winners (spring-training division) were:

- Most-Ogled Outfield Sign: "Hooters Are Wonderful," various ballparks, Florida.
- Best Pun: "The Bug Stops Here," Arab Exterminators, Jack Russell Stadium, Clearwater.
- Best Beer Billboard: "Labatt's Blue Blue Heaven," Grant Field, Dunedin.
- Charm and Innocence Award: "Sweet Baseball," Angels Stadium, Palm Springs.
- Best Home Run Target: Marlboro Man on Horseback or Carrying Saddle, various ballparks, Florida and Arizona.
- Special Effects Award: "Bring it Home" (*Phoenix Gazette*), Phoenix Stadium.
- Foul-Line-to-Foul-Line Award (for overall impact of outfield advertising, with points given for number of signs, quality of art and graphics, and originality): first place, Hi Corbett Field, Tucson; second place, Angels Stadium, Palm Springs; third place (tie), Jack Russell Stadium, Clearwater, and Charlotte County Stadium, Port Charlotte.

Leaf
SWEET BASEBALL
Whoppers
Milk Duds
CLARK
Chuckles
WASTE DISPOSAL SERVICES, INC.
Palm Springs
Keep Our City Clean
Coca-Cola
Find your station in life...
KEZN
FM 103.1

ElderMed·SeniorSave
only at
St. Joseph's

BRADENTON
PITTSBURGH PIRATES
BOOSTERS INC.

TEXAS
Mizuno

STADIUM INFORMATION

Charlotte County Stadium
2300 El Jobean Road
Port Charlotte, FL 33948
(813) 625-9500

How long at present location: Four years
Capacity: 6,026
Dimensions: 340 feet down lines, 410 feet to center
Directions: From U.S. 41, take El Jobean Junction (776 West) toward coast. Stadium is approximately two miles on left.
Parking: Large grass lots, $1.00.

If only these new complexes could have a history transplant, there would be less carping about their newness. The most wonderful icon in Rangers spring lore was the hole that then-rookie phenom Pete Incaviglia drilled through the outfield wall with a line drive at the old park in Pompano Beach. They should have moved that hole to Port Charlotte, Florida, trucked it right across Alligator Alley, and installed it in the new outfield wall. Baseball memories have a short enough shelf life already without taking down the shelves and burning them.

If history *could* be transplanted, the Rangers would certainly have the best ground for it. The field at Charlotte County Stadium is the best in Florida, a sward so green and uniform that it could be mistaken for synthetic if not for the mower-fresh smell. Tim Burns, assistant to Rangers groundskeeper Jimmy Anglia, is the local turfmeister, and it's easy to see why he turned down the Dodger Stadium groundskeeping job: He probably couldn't bear to leave this field behind.

Another Charlotte County plus: A lot of outfield advertising signs. Paint, after all, is history applied with a brush. Buckets of the stuff were used here.

"It's the best facility in spring training, by far," says Tracy Ringolsby of the *Dallas Morning News*. "It's not as plush as the Royals' stadium at Boardwalk and Baseball, but the logistics are better."

Maybe so, but I can't help thinking this stadium would look even better with a hole in the wall.

Ticket Information: box $6.50; reserved $5.50; bleachers $4 (1990 prices). Individual tickets for each game go on sale mid-January, 1991. Telephone and mail orders accepted; each order requires a three-dollar handling charge. Mail orders should include a self-addressed, stamped envelope. Mail ticket requests to Texas Rangers, P.O. Box 3609, Port Charlotte, FL 33949-3609. To order by phone, call (813) 625-9500 or (813) 624-2211. Cash, personal checks, MasterCard, and VISA accepted.

Autograph Opportunities: "The Rangers are super, as good as the Astros," says Lake Worth, Florida, collector Scott Winslow, and most of his fellow collectors seem to agree. "Nolan Ryan is one of the easiest guys and one of the nicest," says collector Tom Bunevich. "It's hard to believe that a big superstar like him is that caliber

SPRING HOME OF THE
Rangers
CHARLOTTE
COUNTY
STADIUM
THIS WEEK
WED - BLUE JAYS
THURS- CARDINALS
TICKETS AVAILABLE
Sarasota Herald-Tribune
CHARLOTTE AM

of a guy. Harold Baines kind of jerks you around and finally does it, but he has a terrible signature, you can't tell whose it is."

Hotels: The Rangers staff lodges at the Palm Island Resort, 7092 Placida Road, Cape Haze, FL 33946; (813) 697-4800. The players who don't have condos stay at the Days Inn–Murdock, 1941 Tamiami Trail, Murdock, FL 33948; (813) 627-8900.

Area Attractions

• Greyhound racing at the **Bonita-Fort Myers Kennel Club**, 10601 Bonita Beach Road (U.S. 41), Bonita Springs. A good half-hour drive from Port Charlotte, but that's nothing when cash is burning a hole in your pocket.

Restaurants, Lounges, and Dives: "There's nothing there," says Rangers outfielder Pete Incaviglia about Port Charlotte. "Zippidy-doo-da. *Zippo.*" Having said that, Incaviglia goes on to give his favorite nothing: "The best place to eat is an Italian joint called Ria's. They have good food." Outfielder Ruben Sierra adds to the Port Charlotte mystique by saying, "My favorite restaurant is my wife. She does all cooking for me." Rangers manager Bobby Valentine, asked for his choice of a good restaurant, says, "Have you ever been to Port Charlotte? I'm going to have to think about this awhile." An hour later, Valentine delivers his decision: "Ria's ain't bad. Little Italy is a good place. But probably the best place in town is Charlie's Raw Bar."

"I probably went to Earl Nightingale's more than anywhere else," says Merle Harmon, the Rangers TV play-by-play man. "It's south of Port Charlotte in Punta Gorda, right on the pier. Earl Nightingale, for many years, was a Chicago radio announcer who did motivational tapes, and he's all over the menu of this place. The food and the decor are very good. I'm a big pompano man, I guess that's my favorite."

> "Something disturbing is going on in Florida. Parodying the rest of the map, ambitious little villages are swiping one another's ballclubs."
>
> —Tom Callahan

"Everything down here is seafood," says Tracy Ringolsby of the *Dallas Morning News*. "I like Nightingale's, and I like Charlie's Raw Bar. The grouper's real good, the wings are good, and the beer is cold."

Chamber of Commerce: (Charlotte County) 2702 Tamiami Trail, Port Charlotte, FL 33952; (813) 627-2222.

Spring Training Sites: 1961–86, Pompano Beach, FL; 1987–present, Port Charlotte.

Won–Lost Record/Attendance:

Year	Record	Attendance
1989	17–11	76,610
1988	15–14–1	70,335
1987	13–16	69,439
1986	15–13	28,402
1985	10–14	23,477

Cactus League

25

STADIUM INFORMATION

Phoenix Municipal Stadium
5999 E. Van Buren
Phoenix, AZ 85008
(602) 225-9400

How long at present location: Ten years
Capacity: 8,500
Dimensions: 345 feet down lines, 390 feet alleys, 410 feet to center
Directions: From I-10 take 48th Street exit east. Road turns into 44th Street. Follow three to four miles to Van Buren; turn right. Follow one mile. Stadium is on right at intersection of Van Buren and Galvin Parkway.
Training site: Scottsdale Community College, 9000 E. Chaparral Road, Scottsdale. (First two weeks of spring training.) From I-10, take University exit east, turn left onto Scottsdale Road. Turn right at Chaparral. SCC is approximately two miles on left.
Parking: Large paved lot, $2.

Rumor has it that Phoenix has a downtown with tall buildings, but this little toe of Phoenix is about as much of the city as Cactus Leaguers ever see. Arizona's spring-training action is centered in the southern and eastern "suburbs" of Scottsdale, Tempe, Mesa, and Chandler—so much so that a day trip to Phoenix proper is a magical mystery tour. The city is worth a look, of course, for its museums, theaters, pro basketball, and what-have-you. For our purposes, though, "Phoenix" is that area within Canseco-blast range of Phoenix Municipal Stadium.

Informality reigns in this handsome ballpark. Blue folding chairs in the boxes allow for strategic repositioning. The press box is open, giving the fans a good look at the ink-stained wretches. (Make that mustard-stained wretches; before the game, the writers eat charcoal-broiled hot dogs and hamburgers in a roped-off media picnic ground down the left-field line.) After the game, it is not unusual to see a gaggle of writers debriefing the A's manager out on the grass, a delightful custom.

The stadium landmark is a rocky butte called Camelback Mountain, out beyond the left-field wall, and there is disagreement about which former A's faces are represented in its natural formations. The face in the tallest rock is definitely that of Dave "Kong" Kingman, who probably chipped the stone himself with some loud fouls.

Ticket Information: Box $8; reserved $6; general admission/grandstand (day of game only) $5. Or write: Oakland Athletics, Phoenix Municipal Stadium, 5999 E. Van Buren, Phoenix, AZ 85008.

Autograph Opportunities: "The parking lot is the best place to get the A's, except for Jose Canseco," says University of Colorado student Jeff Ashworth. "Jose gets his wife to drive his Corvette inside the gate when it's time to leave, so he won't have to sign. But all the kids pile up against the gate and won't let him leave."

"Canseco won't sign, that's for sure," agrees

Ashworth's college chum, Mike Fox of Minneapolis. "It's always 'After the game.' "

"The A's are very difficult," says Joe Miller of Sports America, a card shop in Mesa. "Access isn't easy, and last year they added a lot of security because of the mobs that showed up to see the pennant winners. Dave Stewart is pretty decent. Canseco and McGwire are okay during games; they'll walk along the fence and sign, but after the game it's very difficult."

"I get a lot of feedback from people who come into the store," says Rich Willie, co-owner of Baseball Cards Plus in Mesa. "This is hearsay, but I hear that Reggie Jackson messed up a couple of balls for kids by writing 'Popeye' or 'Johnny Carson.' Other times, though, he would sit down and sign for an hour. It depends on the mood he's in."

Team Hotel: Doubletree Suites, 320 N. 44th St., Phoenix, AZ 85008; (602) 225-0500. Also close to the stadium is the Seattle Mariners' team hotel, the Sheraton Tempe Mission Palms Hotel, 60 E. 5th St., in Old Town Tempe.

Area Attractions

• The **Hall of Flame** firefighting museum. Adjacent to Phoenix Stadium, this warehouse-type structure houses the world's largest exhibit of firefighting trucks and pumpers, including equipment from the eighteenth century. Admission: $3 adults; $2 senior citizens; $1 children; no charge for children under six. Open Monday-Saturday, 9: A.M. to 5:00 P.M., (602) ASK-FIRE.

• **The Phoenix Zoo.** Another Phoenix Stadium neighbor (5810 E. Van Buren), the zoo bills itself as the city's "most popular attraction" with more than a million visitors a year. More than 1,200 animals on exhibit, including nearly 200 endangered animals. The Children's Zoo includes a petting zoo and an animal nursery. Open every day, 9:00 A.M. to 5:00 P.M. Adults $5; children five to twelve $2; no charge for children under four.

• **Old Town Tempe.** On Mill Avenue between Phoenix Stadium and Arizona State University, this commercial district is Tempe's answer to Old Scottsdale. Dozens of shops, restaurants, nightclubs, and commercial services in restored, turn-of-the-century buildings.

• **Desert Botanical Garden.** More than 10,000 varieties of desert pricklies and flora, including a three-acre permanent exhibit, "Plants and People of the Sonoran Desert." Open daily, 9:00 A.M. until sunset. Adults $3; children 50 cents; children under five free. Near Phoenix

> "For me, Arizona baseball is personified by a young woman vendor at Phoenix Stadium I came to recognize, after several springs, by her call. She would slowly make her way down an aisle carrying her basket and then sing out a gentle, musical '*Hot* dog! . . . *Hot* dog!'—a half note and then down four steps to a whole note. She'd go away, and later you heard the same pausing, repeated cry at a different distance, like the cry of a single bird working the edge of a meadow on a warm summer afternoon. '*Hot* dog!' "
>
> —Roger Angell

Stadium in Papago Park, 1201 North Galvin Parkway.

• Greyhound racing at the **New Greyhound Park,** East Washington at 40th Street, Phoenix.

• **The Heard Museum**, 22 E. Monte Vista Road, Phoenix, features 75,000 artifacts of Native American life. For information about special events and exhibits, call (602) 252-8848. Open year round. Adults $3; senior citizens $2.50; students and children over seven $1; Native Americans and children under seven, free.

Restaurants, Lounges, and Dives: In addition to the Pink Pony and the other Scottsdale favorites, the A's entourage patronizes Steamer's, Tony Roma's, Studebaker's, and the Sports Page (a neighborhood sports bar with very good ribs). "There's a place off Lincoln Drive," says A's slugger Mark McGwire, "an old-houselike thing called the Lodge. This place has the all-time best deep-fried lobster, and they serve gooey-buns with their salad. I also like Oscar Taylor's, which is right in the mall at 24th and Camelback. The bakery is right in the restaurant, and they serve great rolls and Danish and stuff."

Catcher Ron Hassey and *San Francisco Chronicle* writer Dave Bush recommend Riazzi's Italian Gardens, a spot that was popular with the San Francisco Giants before the A's discovered it. "It's real old-fashioned Italian," says Bush. "Eggplant, pasta, spaghetti and meatballs. It's not fettuccine with pine nuts."

A's executive vice president Roy Eisenhardt: "To be honest, I take my young kids to spring training, and we go to McDonald's a lot."

And pitcher Mike Moore, who lives in the area, shakes his head when asked where he'd take visitors from out of town: "Probably nowhere. I'm in the back yard, barbecuing."

Chambers of Commerce: Greater Paradise Valley: 16042 N. 32nd St., Suite B-1A, Phoenix, AZ 85032; (602) 482-3344. Phoenix Metro: 34 W. Monroe St., Suite 900, Phoenix, AZ 85003; (602) 254-5521.

Spring Training Sites: 1968, Bradenton, FL; 1969–78, Mesa; 1979–81, Scottsdale; 1982–present, Phoenix.

Won-Lost Record/Attendance:

Year	Record	Attendance
1989	19–13	94,866
1988	14–16	85,587
1987	14–15	61,470
1986	17–12	45,158
1985	13–13–1	31,072

Nico Pemantle (right) and KALX engineer Phil Rainey

Rookie at the Mike

It's the late innings of an A's-Brewers game at Phoenix Municipal Stadium, and play-by-play announcer Nico Pemantle has barely had time to digest four defensive changes when he spots number 70 on the back of the new Milwaukee pitcher.

"Spring-training nightmare," Nico mutters, thumbing through the Brewers media guide. "He's not on the roster!"

In the few seconds before he goes back on the air to the San Francisco Bay area, Nico's engineer, Phil Rainey, slips him a one-word note—"NAVARRO"—and rushes out of the booth for more information. Nico resumes his play-by-play with only that half-name and one other hard fact: The new hurler is a right-hander.

It's "wing-it" time on KALX.

"Navarro gives you a lot of his number, *à la* Luis Tiant," Nico tells his listeners, calmly splitting his attention between the field and his hand-drawn scorecard. "Breaking ball down low, and it's one and oh . . . " Rainey is soon back with the dope on Navarro, and before the second out of the inning Nico is casually reeling off Navarro's minor-league numbers. Like a shortstop handling a bad-hop grounder, Nico has made the play.

"Fast ball spotted on the outside corner, ball two . . . "

Spring baseball, with its lineup juggling and unfamiliar players, is tough enough for the veteran broadcaster, but Nico Pemantle is still in college. His station, KALX, is the campus voice of the University of California, Berkeley. That makes Nico the radio equivalent of a baseball number 70—a prospect trying out for the bigs. "My dream," he says between innings, "is definitely to be a baseball play-by-play announcer."

Nico is something of a spring phenom. When Dave Parker smashes a two-run homer off the scoreboard in right-center, giving the A's a 3-1 lead, the kid announcer tests his narrative skills: "So, Parker's bomb puts a buzz in the crowd that will probably last the rest of the half-inning. That bounced off the scoreboard and *changed* the scoreboard by two runs." On other plays, he shows himself to be observant ("Lansford is well up on the grass at third base because Felder likes to bunt") and alert for the unexpected ("Look out! That's going back to the screen, a breaking ball behind Meyer. The runner will take third").

"I started broadcasting baseball games in my head when I was eight or nine," Nico says after the game, sitting in an empty box behind the visitors' dugout. "I used to sit in the center-field bleachers in the Oakland Coliseum and talk into a tape recorder. The first inning, people used to stare at me. The second inning, people would try to distract me by making jokes or calling the game themselves. By the third inning, they'd be *listening.* "

Now he practices in real broadcast booths, both as Cal baseball's "Voice of the Bears" and as KALX's Cactus League hotshot. "A college station sending someone to do spring-training baseball is unheard of," Nico says. "I'm really lucky."

If so, he made his own luck. When he was a freshman, Nico noticed that KSFO, the Bay Area station with rights to the A's games, broadcast only the weekend spring games. He took a demo tape of himself doing an inning of A's baseball to the A's director of broadcasting and said, "I can put this on the air for you if you want." The director said yes, so Nico paid his own way to Arizona and made his big-league debut in the spring of 1987.

"The first spring game is always tough because I haven't done it for a year," he admits. "I do Bears baseball, but there's nothing quite like a major-league game with major-league pressure."

Nico's heroes are the Bay Area broadcasters he listened to while growing up—Lon Simmons, Bill King, and Hank Greenwald. "Lon Simmons joined me in the booth for a half-inning last year, and my heart was pounding 200 beats a minute. I can't put into words how much I respect him. His personality is enviable, his play-by-play is crisp." Nico grins. "I even have a shirt with his picture on it."

STADIUM INFORMATION

Scottsdale Stadium
7402 East Osborn Road
Scottsdale, AZ 85251
(602) 990-7972

How long at present location: Ten years
Capacity: 5,300
Dimensions: 360 feet down lines, 430 feet to center
Directions: Two blocks east of North Scottsdale Road at the intersection of Osborne and Civic Center Drive. Take I-10 to Scottsdale Road exit, head north to Osborn and turn right. Stadium is on left.
Training site: Indian School Park, intersection of Hayden and Camelback Road, Scottsdale (three blocks east of North Scottsdale Road and about a mile north of Scottsdale Stadium).
Parking: Pay parking at various lots east of stadium, $2 to $3; free parking (limited space) in Civic Center garage north of stadium.

Scottsdale Stadium is one of spring baseball's most charming structures . . . from the outside. A combination of artful landscaping and redwood siding gives the place a cool and woodsy look as you file in. And the neighborhood is great, too—right next to the law courts in the Civic Center and within walking distance of Old Scottsdale's shops and restaurants. There is even a cactus garden between the sidewalk and the wall behind the left-field bleachers—a great place to pose your prickly in-laws for a snapshot.

Inside, the charm is dissipated by the playing field's absurdly gargantuan dimensions—360 feet down the lines, 414 feet in the power alleys, and 430 feet to center. Cactus League parks tend to be spacious because the ball carries well in the dry desert air, but from the Scottsdale grandstand the advertising on the outfield walls is practically unreadable without binoculars. What's worse, the base paths aren't so close either, robbing the park of the intimacy promised from the outside. A sharp operator could probably make a fortune developing Scottsdale Stadium's wasted space into diamond-view condominiums.

Go anyway. Scottsdale is the vibrant center of Cactus League baseball, the place where the baseball community gathers after dark to renew friendships and swap outrageous lies. Old Scottsdale is the best place to grab a meal, buy a painting, or just go for a stroll. (You'll see more Brewers, Cubs, and Mariners walking with their families on North Scottsdale Avenue than you'll see at any one place in Chandler, Mesa, or Tempe.) And, of course, Scottsdale is where you'll find the legendary Pink Pony (see sidebar).

If you're a Giants fan, so much the better.

Ticket Information: box $6; reserved $5; general admission bleachers $4. Season and single-game tickets on sale January 1. For tickets, call (602) 994-5123 or write to Scottsdale Charros, Box 1573, Scottsdale, AZ 85251.

Autograph Opportunities: "Scottsdale is maybe the best place in Arizona to get auto-

SF
SAN FRANCISCO
LEAGUE BASEBALL
CUBS

graphs," says Jeff Ashworth of Andover, Mass. "Scottsdale and Chandler. All the Giants come out the same door and the parking lot is real close." "The Giants are pretty easy," agrees Joe Miller of Sports America in Mesa. "There's no security around. Will Clark, it depends on what day it is. The majority of the time, he's a tough autograph. Kevin Mitchell is almost impossible. Willie Mays is pretty decent, believe it or not. He's a very grumpy person when he signs at a show, but here he's representing the Giants and he's more cheerful about it. He'll stop and sign about a dozen."

Mike Fox, a University of Colorado student from Minneapolis, says that he was waiting outside the Giants clubhouse door two springs ago when a tall fellow in sunglasses came out carrying a huge stack of cartons that hid his face. "He got all the way to the parking lot before the little kids recognized that it was Will Clark," Fox says with a laugh. "He was cool."

Team Hotel: Sheraton Scottsdale Resort, 7200 North Scottsdale Road, Scottsdale, AZ 85253; (602) 948-5000. Another popular baseball hostelry is the Sunburst Hotel at 4959 North Scottsdale Road, Scottsdale, Arizona 85251; (602) 945-7666. Water basketball and late-afternoon croquet are part of the Sunburst ambiance, and the place is a favorite of well-heeled writers and baseball executives.

"The Hyatt Regency-Gainey Ranch in Scottsdale is the most amazing hotel complex I've ever seen," says *Washington Post* baseball writer Tom Boswell. "It's like Aku-Aku plus waterfalls. You go there for a drink. You don't stay there—God knows how much it costs. The place must have a hundred swimming pools, all different shapes. If you pulled off the back of a radio and exposed all the little wafers, wires, and terminals, that's what an aerial view would look like. But instead of cathodes, it's palm trees, swimming pools, and big stone statues. You go there, pay five dollars for a drink, and say, 'Holy ——! What is this?' "

Area Attractions

- **Old Scottsdale.** Billed as "the West's most western town," this downtown shopping district is a short walk from the ballpark and draws on its 1880s origins, but the ambiance is closer to Rodeo Drive than to Boot Hill. It's a window-shopper's pig-out with more than 150 shops and restaurants. Art lovers should not overlook the dozens of galleries lining both sides of Main Street on the west side of Scottsdale Road.
- **Arizona State University** baseball. The Sun Devils play their home games at beautiful Packard Stadium, just down the road in Tempe. For schedule and ticket information, call (602) 965-2381.

Restaurants, Lounges, and Dives: Scottsdale is the night-life capital of spring baseball and the home of the legendary Pink Pony. "I'd never think of going to Arizona without going to the Pony," says Cubs broadcaster Harry Caray. "The Pony is like that place on television, Cheers," says former National League president Chub Feeney. "You go where they know you."

Not far behind the Pony in terms of Cactus Leaguer's loyalty is Don and Charlie's, a great steak and rib joint. Other Giants favorites include Tony Roma's (ribs), Trader Vic's (quasi-Polynesian-Oriental), and the sneakily named Pink Pepper (a Thai restaurant). "Not all of these places, one should be warned, are joints," writes *Sports Illustrated*'s Ron Fimrite. "With Scottsdale emerging as a sort of Carmel East or Provincetown West, the city fairly bulges with quaint boites with menus in French and waiters in tuxedos."

Until last year, that pretty much described Steven's, an elegant and highly regarded gourmet restaurant owned by former Cy Young–winning pitcher Steve Stone. Steven's is now Harry

AISLE 2
SECTIONS
BOX B & C
RESERVED
GRANDSTAND
SECTIONS
D E F
GIANTS

& Steve's, a companion to the popular Mesa sports bar owned by Stone and his Cubs broadcasting partner, Harry Caray. Says Stone: "We knocked out a couple of walls, took out the velvet booths, put in more vinyl, put in a skylight, put baseball memorabilia on the walls, and installed big-screen TVs to make it a Chicago-style sports bar. Our salads are wonderful, and we have probably the best hamburgers in the city." Both Harry and Steve say they now spend more time at the Scottsdale location than at the original Harry & Steve's in Mesa.

For those whose taste runs more to coffee ice cream than to Irish coffee, the best Cactus League ice cream parlor is also in Scottsdale: the Sugar Bowl on the corner of North Scottsdale Road and First Avenue, a few steps north of the Pony.

Chamber of Commerce: 7333 Scottsdale Mall, Scottsdale, AZ 85251-4498; (602) 945-8481.

Spring Training Sites: 1958–80, Phoenix; 1981–present, Scottsdale.

> "Certainly it's old stuff, this spring training, and has been going on for about a century now, from the time ballplayers wore long woolen sweaters over their uniforms instead of windbreakers. Yet spring training is always new—a time of rebirth, of rejuvenation, of refurbishing, of breaking out the spitballs from the mothballs."
>
> —Ira Berkow

Won-Lost Record/Attendance:

Year	Record	Attendance
1989	13–19	56,095
1988	16–14	61,223
1987	20–10	54,392
1986	15–12	61,469
1985	14–14-1	58,328

'Hidden Talent' Ray Stella

Most visitors to Scottsdale Stadium do a double-take when they walk by beer vendor Ray Stella's concession stand. The cartoons on the counter catch the eye—funny baseball sketches with captions such as, "Beat those A's!" and "Chicago Cubs? Never heard of 'em!"

"I'm doing this as a lark," Stella explains between innings—referring, apparently, to the beer business. "I'm in the book, *Hidden Talents of Phoenix.*" He produces a card: RAY STELLA, CARTOONIST. YOUR HOBBIES, LIKES, DISLIKES CREATED FROM YOUR INITIALS, ADDRESS, ETC.

Tearing a page off a beer order pad, Stella says, "Give me your initials." Wielding a felt marker, he writes "JSG" vertically, like a totem pole with G on the bottom. He looks up. "What's your hobby?"

Given "piano playing," Stella frowns and turns the paper this way and that. "Do you see a piano in there?" Finally, he settles on the letters in the upside-down position and begins to sketch. In less than thirty seconds, working around the initials, he has a likeness of his subject bent over a keyboard. A quickly scrawled title: "Big John at the Ivories."

"There you go," he says. "No charge."

So quick is Stella the cartoonist that he normally charges by the hour, not by the sketch. "I

Cartoonist-vendor Ray Stella

do birthday parties, weddings, bar mitzvahs—anything up to a couple of hundred people. I once did 250 cartoons in four hours for an All-state Insurance meeting."

Stella did not set out to be either a cartoonist or a beer vendor. He started drawing when he was four years old and had ambitions as a serious artist. "I don't want to brag or anything, but I had a natural talent. I attended the Art Institute of Chicago and spent two years at the Chicago Academy of Fine Arts."

So why the career change? He shrugs. "You have to be dead fifty years for anybody to enjoy your work. I went into cartooning instead, and it took over."

Stella claims as his own the idea of making cartoons from people's initials. "I can see the cartoon right away. It doesn't matter if it's Chinese characters or Arabic or hieroglyphics. I've always had that gift. I look up in a tree, and I see figures in the leaves."

When he isn't working parties as a sketch artist, Stella takes on more conventional assignments—sort of. "I drew all the cartoons for the book *How Not to Pay Your Bills.* It's a book about avoiding your creditors."

A Baseball Scribe's View of the Pink Pony

Some years back, Roger Angell of *The New Yorker* called the Pink Pony "the best baseball restaurant in the land." Those words got Angell quoted (and caricatured) in *Sports Illustrated,* when his good friend Ron Fimrite wrote his own piece on the legendary Scottsdale hangout. Now Fimrite and Angell are cited whenever someone mentions the Pony, which only proves that the shortest route to immortality, for the modern writer, is to immoderately praise a favorite hangout. (Are you listening, Calvin Trillin?)

Either writer qualifies as a world-renowned expert on the Pony. Angell, concerned that the Pony has already gotten too much attention for its own good, said last spring, "Tell your readers that it's overrated and too crowded and they won't like it." He said this, however, while driving to the Pony for dinner.

Fimrite, too, said he discourages all but the most garrulous and good-natured folk from dropping into the Pony, but he graciously agreed to be questioned about his favorite haunt.

Q: Who goes to the Pony and why?
A: Well, the Pony has been there for forty-odd years. For many years it was about the only place in town. Charlie Briley took it over around 1950, back when the Cactus League was getting started. Dizzy Dean was a great hunting buddy of his, and Dean used to tell stories about Charlie on his "Game of the Week" telecasts. In no time at all, the Pink Pony became the place to go for people who wanted to talk about baseball.

The players, of course, don't really eat out that much anymore. They live in condos and their families are with them . . . or their mistresses. But in the old days, the ballplayers used to go to the Pony constantly, as did the managers and coaches and everybody connected with baseball. Because of that, the writers started going there also, and over not-so-many years it became an absolute hangout. I knew about the Pony long before I ever saw it, and I've been coming here regularly for eighteen years and several times before that.

Q: Is there a Florida hangout that compares to it?
A: There's no place anywhere that compares to it. Certainly not in Florida, because the Florida teams are too spread out. What you have here are five teams in the same place; seven teams really, for the Angels and Padres are here for the

At the Pink Pony—Roger Angell (left), Linda Fimrite, and Ron Fimrite

first three or four weeks. I guess the only rival the Pony has is a place here called Don and Charlie's, which has become a sort of hangout, but certainly no place has commanded baseball people's loyalty for as long as the Pony. Even in major cities you don't have a place where so many baseball people come to talk and have a good time. It's become so god-damned popular, now it's hard to get into.

Q: What is the "power table"?
A: There's one really large booth in the main dining room, back in the righthand corner. It's the largest booth in the place, and I guess you'd call it the power table. The other night, for example, three National League presidents, past and present, were there for dinner— Bart Giamatti, Bill White, and Chub Feeney.

Q: Where do you like to sit?
A: I like the smaller booths in the bar. You're closer to the action there. Except if it's a large group, I would prefer, naturally, the power booth.

Q: Who might one see if one visits the Pony on a typical spring night?
A: On a regular basis you can count on seeing a lot of broadcasters and writers from all over the country. A lot of old ballplayers. There was one night they had five Hall of Fame players in the same booth—Mickey Mantle, Lou Boudreau, Bob Lemon, Eddie Mathews, and Ernie Banks. Billy Martin, when he was managing the A's, was there every single night. Don Sutton rarely missed a night when he was with the Angels. Of the current players, Will Clark of the Giants goes there a lot, usually with one of his teammates.

You can definitely count on any number of scouts. Walt Dropo has been in. I don't even know if he's in baseball now, but he was in the Pony. John McNamara, the manager, has been in. Chub Feeney is a regular. Bill Rigney you can count on. A lot of the Oakland staff and P.R. people. And you'll see every one of the managers in there at least one night.

Q: What's the story with the framed caricatures on the walls?
A: That goes way back. Ted Williams is on that wall.

Q: So is Ron Fimrite.
A: *(Embarrassed)* Oh, well. The ones from the fifties were done by Don Barclay, who was a Walt Disney animator, but he died. The later ones were done by Charlie's wife, Gwen. Rigney, you'll notice, is depicted as a player or as a young manager—very serious and dark-haired. The latest addition is Roger Angell. He went up night before last.

Q: The food?
A: One of the charms of the place is that the food is really excellent. It's a steakhouse, but there are other things. I've been eating the broiled shrimp, and I love it. The service is good, too. Charlie and Gwen are very careful about who they hire, and the level of efficiency is better than you'll find at most major restaurants. The bartenders are extraordinary.

Q: But the principal appeal of the place is that it's a great place to go and talk.
A: Yeah, that's basically it. Any great place, that's why you go there. The food at the Pony is excellent, the service is good, the drinks are full . . . but the real measure of a hangout is the conversation.

(The Pink Pony, 3831 N. Scottsdale Road, Scottsdale, AZ 85251; (602) 945-6697 or 949-8677.)

CHICAGO
SOUVENIRS
CUBS
SPRING TRAINING
CHICAGO CUBS
HOHOKAM BALL PARK
MESA, ARIZONA
CHICAGO
ATHLETICS FAN PARKING ONLY

STADIUM INFORMATION

HoHoKam Park
1235 North Center Street
Mesa, AZ 85201
(602) 461-0061

How long at present location: Twelve years
Capacity: 8,927
Dimensions: 350 feet down lines, 400 feet to center
Directions: From Tucson, I-10 North to Superstition Highway (360 East), exit north on Country Club Drive; turn right at Brown Road; turn left at Center. Ballpark is one block on the right. From Tempe or Mesa, take any major east-west street to Country Club, turn north, and follow directions above. From Chandler, take Arizona Avenue (87 North); it becomes Country Club Drive in Mesa.
Parking: Paved and grass.

Jim Frey, the Chicago Cubs director of baseball operations (and former manager), leaned back in the Cubs dugout one day and passed judgment on the Arizona lifestyle. "Jesus, it's gorgeous," he said to no one in particular. "I wake up in the morning, the sun is shining, there's a golf course and a lake in front of me, and I say, 'What could be better than this?' "

Apparently, a lot of Cubs fans agree with Frey. Midwesterners have been retiring to the Phoenix area in droves (actually, in Oldsmobiles), and many of them are Cubs fanatics. HoHoKam Park has been expanded, expanded, and expanded again, and still the old folks pack its unshaded aluminum bleachers to root for their beloved Cubbies. Every game is a sellout. When the Cubs play at Phoenix, Tempe, or Scottsdale, those games are usually sellouts, too.

The expansions have robbed HoHoKam of what little charm it possessed. The first-base-side bleachers, twenty-five rows deep, run all the way to the left-field wall like the student section in a small-college football stadium. The chain-link outfield fence is backed by bushes, as if to suggest ivy without actually having ivy. The grandstand itself is a squarish pile of cinder block more suited to an industrial site than the pleasant suburban park it dominates.

And yet, the place *is* charming, once it's filled with Cubs fans. No other spring-training park attracts as many rabid, knowledgeable, and vocal baseball nuts. (HoHoKam has more than its share of shrill-voiced ladies with blue hair who call manager Don Zimmer "Sweetie" and shout advice during the game.) The old loyalists carry many wounds to the heart from previous campaigns, and they follow the Cubs with the edgy obsessiveness of jilted lovers.

"I think Cubs fans are the greatest," says autograph hound Jeff Ashworth of Andover, Mass. "You see 150-year-old guys with their beards dyed blue."

You also see kids at HoHoKam, but you can bet they're grandchildren.

Ticket Information: At press time, the Cubs had not yet released their 1991 ticket prices. Last year's prices were grandstand $6; outfield grandstand (first base) $5; bleachers (third base)

$3.50. For current prices and information, call (602) 964-4467 or write to "The HoHoKams," P.O. Box 261, Mesa, AZ 85201.

Autograph Opportunities: "The Cubs are easy," says Joe Miller, who works at his father's card shop in Mesa. "My little sister went down there and got every single Cub in one day, no problem. Of course, she's eight years old and female. We even have players come into the store and sign. Darrin Jackson was in this year. Jim Frey comes in all the time. His wife buys things, T-shirts for the grandkids. They don't get them at the park—too expensive there, he says. Frey looks at the old cards, the guys he played with."

"I like going for announcers and ex-ballplayers," says Jeff Ashworth. "Harry Caray was really cool. He signed my baseball 'Holy cow!' "

Team Hotel: Mazona Motor Hotel, 250 West Main St., Mesa, AZ 85201; (602) 834-9233. Harry Caray stays at the Ambassador Hotel in Scottsdale.

Area Attractions

- The **Mesa Southwest Museum:** history of the Southwest from the dinosaurs to the Old West. In downtown Mesa at 53 North Macdonald.

• The **Arizona Museum for Youth** in downtown Mesa. One of only two museums in the country that allow children to experience art through hands-on activities.
• **Saquaro Lake.** Marina, fishing, swimming, and other water sports. Excursions on the forty-six passenger paddleboat, *Desert Belle,* (602) 837-9709.
• **The Superstition Mountains,** site of the legendary "Lost Dutchman" gold mine. Horseback riding, hiking, picnic areas. For information and trail maps, contact the Tonto National Forest Service, (602) 835-1161.
• Greyhound racing at **Apache Greyhound Park,** Apache Junction.

Restaurants, Lounges, and Dives: Mesa is home to the original Harry & Steve's, a Chicago-style sports bar owned by former Cy Young Award–winner Steve Stone and Hall of Fame broadcaster Harry Caray. ("You remember what Skip Caray said about Harry?" asks Jim Frey. " 'In many ways he's been like a father to me.' ") Mesa is also, according to baseball sabermetrician and author Bill James, home to a really good meatball sandwich. "My favorite place is about three blocks from HoHoKam Park—a drive-through, there's always a line of cars—but I can't remember its name. Great meatball sandwiches."

"I'm a big Don and Charlie's freak," says columnist Bob Verdi of the *Chicago Tribune.* "Don Carson is a Chicago guy, and he's done the place in kind of a Chicago motif. I wouldn't call it a sports bar, but there must be a million pennants on the wall, and damn, the place is packed.

> "Sweat is overrated. In the old days, when players came into spring training ten pounds overweight, maybe you liked Florida more because of the humidity. You perspire more, you shed the excess. But now, these guys come into camp ready, or at least they should be. You get your work in and you don't need to sweat."
>
> —Don Zimmer, Cubs manager

Ribs, chicken, good hospitality—Don makes sure it's always upbeat and friendly; he's a very warm guy. I think the best endorsement is that Don and Charlie's is a busy place even in July, when Scottsdale slows to a crawl."

Chamber of Commerce: 120 N. Center St., Mesa, AZ 85201; (602) 969-1307.

Spring Training Sites: 1921–41, Catalina Island, CA; 1942–44, French Lick, IN; 1945–51, Catalina Island, CA; 1952–65, Mesa; 1966, Long Beach, CA; 1967–78, Scottsdale; 1979–present, Mesa.

Won-Lost Record/Attendance:

Year	Record	Attendance
1989	9–23	126,205
1988	17–17	130,584
1987	19–14	106,313
1986	13–22	101,055
1985	18–13–1	102,950

360
KNOCK

STADIUM INFORMATION

Tempe Diablo Stadium
2200 West Alameda
Tempe, AZ 85282
(602) 438-8803

How long at present location: Fifteen years
Capacity: 5,600
Dimensions: 360 feet down lines, 420 feet in power alleys, 430 feet to center
Directions: From I-10, take Broadway exit, go west on Broadway to 48th St., turn left. Stadium is half-mile down; turn left at Alameda.
Parking: Paved.

Tempe Diablo Stadium is not so much a place as it is a location, in the Hollywood sense of the word. That sprawling structure up in the knobby buttes behind the ballpark looks like the secret mountain research laboratory in a fifties sci-fi movie, and the landscape in most other directions is straight out of *Treasure of the Sierra Madre.* From the parking lot, a path up the hillside leads to an attractive brick-and-stucco arcade of Mediterranean cast, suggesting that grapes, and not the Mariners, are being stomped within. *Sports Illustrated*'s Ron Fimrite once wrote that Tempe Diablo looks "like someplace the Magnificent Seven might have been called upon to defend."

No wonder, then, that game-day tickets are sold out of a trailer in the parking lot. You expect somebody to yell, "Strike the set!" and haul the whole business off by nightfall.

It's a lovely park, really, once you get inside. Simple and clean—*very* clean—and possessed of an intimacy that seems to come with natural-bowl stadia. Down the third-base line, a grass hillside invites those with good memories of Woodstock to unfurl blankets and trade witticisms with the Mariners bullpen.

For years this has been the easiest ticket in the Cactus League, but attendance jumped by 20,000 between 1987 and 1989, suggesting that the crowds are starting to follow the path of least resistance. "The growing trend is to get your tickets early," warns one Mariners official.

That secret mountain research laboratory, by the way, is no laboratory—it's a hotel. No telling what goes on there, though.

Ticket Information: At press time, the Mariners had not released their 1991 ticket prices. Tickets go on sale in January and may be ordered in writing (Seattle Mariners, Tempe Diablo Stadium, 2200 West Alameda, Tempe, AZ 85282) or by calling the ticket office, (602) 438-8900.

Autograph Opportunities: "I hear Ken Griffey, Jr., was really an ace this year; signed anything and was real nice about it," says Rich Willie, co-owner of Baseball Cards Plus in Mesa. "The Mariners might be the nicest guys of all," adds collector Jeff Ashworth. "Harold Reynolds even lets you put your arm around him for a picture."

The security people at Tempe Diablo Stadium are surprisingly tolerant of youngsters who crawl out on the dugout roofs for autographs

> "Whoever called this place Paradise Valley was trying to sell it. Arizona looks like somebody swept all the debris of the United States down into one corner."
>
> —Bernie Linicome, *Chicago Tribune*

during batting and fielding practice. "Maybe they're happy just to get the fans out there," suggests Mesa's Joe Miller of Sports America.

A favorite area with autograph hounds is the grassy hill down the left-field line, right by the Mariners bullpen. Says Ashworth, "You get tons of balls there, too, during batting practice."

Team Hotel: Sheraton Tempe Mission Palms Hotel, 60 E. 5th St., Tempe, AZ 85281; (602) 894-1400. (Attention A's fans: This slick new hotel is also convenient to Phoenix Municipal Stadium.) Other Tempe hotels popular with fans include the Ramada Inn (where the Mariners used to stay), the Point Resort at South Mountain, and the Marriott Courtyard near the airport. The Mariners' owner, George Argyros, stays at the top-of-the-line Westcourt in the Buttes—that secret mountain research lab behind Tempe Diablo Stadium. Baseball author and numbers-cruncher Bill James: "I stay at a little place on the highway—Apache Boulevard—on that strip of motels with flashing lights and neon cactuses. I can't remember its name, but it's across the street from Pizza Hut, right near ASU."

Area Attractions

• **Arizona State University,** Tempe. College baseball at Packard Stadium, performing arts at Frank Lloyd Wright's startling Gammage Center, and all the other excitements of a major college campus. For information on campus events, call (602) 965-2381.

• **Old Town Tempe Festival of the Arts,** March 20-April 1. One of the country's largest and best arts and crafts fairs. For information, call the Mill Avenue Merchants' Association at (602) 967-4877.

Restaurants, Lounges, and Dives: Two places within walking distance of the Sheraton get a lot of Mariner business: Monti's La Casa Vieja has been serving great steaks for forty years; and Mill Landing features fresh seafood flown in daily. Another popular spot is the Rustler's Roost in the Point at South Mountain. For night life, the younger players like the hangouts around Arizona State University, particularly Studebaker's.

"Studebaker's is more for the yuppie, twenty-ish crowd," says Andi Levin, a recent graduate of Arizona State University. "They have a great happy hour. There's also a place right next to the ballpark called Top of the Rocks in Westcourt in the Buttes. The drinks are expensive, but they have a great band. There's a new place called McDuff's. It's huge, TV screens everywhere. It's right down the street from ASU, and it's *the* college sports bar. There's also the Dash Inn on Apache, which is *the* college place. There's a saying at the Dash—'You dash in and crawl out.' It's a very rowdy, Joe College kind of place. It's a dive, actually, but the owners are the nicest people."

Chamber of Commerce: 60 E. 5th St., Tempe, AZ 85281; (602) 967-7891.

Spring Training Sites: 1976–present, Tempe.

Won–Lost Record/Attendance:

Year	Record	Attendance
1989	16–15	60,513
1988	15–15	55,824
1987	13–15	40,515
1986	12–16–1	27,855
1985	12–16–1	30,221

TICKETS
FOR
TODAY'S GAME
ARE ON SALE
AT THE TRAILER
PARKING LOT
LEVEL →

7

STADIUM INFORMATION

Compadre Stadium
1425 West Ocotillo Road
Chandler, AZ 85245
(602) 821-2100

How long at present location: Five years
Capacity: 5,000 (plus grass seating)
Dimensions: 335 feet down lines, 404 feet to center
Directions: From Phoenix, I-10 South to Chandler Boulevard, east to Price Road, turn south on Price to Ocotillo development, follow signs to stadium. From Tucson, I-10 North, exit Riggs Road, head east to Alma School Road, turn left and drive three miles. Ballpark will be on left side. From Tempe or Mesa, take any major east-west street to Alma School Road, head south, and look for signs to ballpark.
Parking: Grass lots, plentiful.

No looming ballpark here. Compadre Stadium is a desert rodent's lair, buried in rolling terrain in Chandler's most rural extremities. Since you can't see the field from the parking lot, you'll feel like you're arriving at a polo match or a golf tournament. (Plenty of high handicappers are visible on the fairways of the adjacent Ocotillo Country Club, part of the Ocotillo development.)

It's a long walk to the stadium gates, but a pleasant one. The sidewalk winds through a grassy park, where ballplayers work out behind chain-link fences, and then rides the rim of the stadium bowl from the outfield around to the stadium gates.

The stadium itself, opened in 1986, is a little gem of post-modern simplicity: low-lined, clean, and tastefully painted in two shades of gray with blue trim. The grassy banks behind the outfield fences provide a lush backdrop for baseball, and when the crowds are big the grass is opened up for spectators. Beautiful.

Bleacher-types may find Compadre a bit sterile—too new, too pristine. And yes, a game here is a little like a concert-on-the-lawn with the philharmonic. But hey, beautiful music is beautiful music, whether it comes from a bassoon or a bat.

Ticket Information: At press time, the Brewers had not yet released their 1991 ticket prices. Last year's prices were grand box $6.50; box $5.50; reserved grandstand $4.50; grass seating $3.50 (day of game only). Season and single-game ticket orders taken beginning in December, payment by check only. Write to Ticket Information, Compadre Stadium, 3800 South Alma School Road, Chandler, AZ 85248, or call (602) 895-1200. Tickets will be held at "will call"

> "I have given up trying to convince friends and acquaintances that covering spring training is hard work, even though it is. Sometimes it takes a half-hour to get a pitcher of lemonade poolside, and choosing the proper sunscreen filter is a constant challenge."
>
> —Scott Ostler, *The National*

AN INTERVIEW WITH BREWERS TRAINER JOHN ADAM

Q. You used to hear stories about ballplayers reporting to spring training overweight and out of shape.
A. Not any longer. I've been the trainer here for nine years, and I'd be hard pressed to think of someone who showed up for major league spring training needing to play his way into shape. That way of thinking went out with the hula hoop.

Q. Why the change?
A. With today's salaries, players don't have to work in the off-season, so they can devote more time to their profession, which is baseball. We give the players October off for R-and-R, but November and December are devoted to building back their strength, which is beaten down during the course of the season. When we test them in December, our worst fears are usually realized: their strength is down and their body fat is significantly up. But they should be making solid strength gains.

On January 1, we tell them to taper down to specific exercises, such as the light dumbbells, to strengthen the cuff up or help the elbow. That's when guys begin to throw again, pitchers and position-players alike.

Q. What happens when they report to you in Chandler?
A. We test them on the Cybex machines for flexibility, strength, and endurance. We get a baseline for the new players and it gives us a comparison for the veterans. Of course, you usually have three or four guys who are post-op that you've been monitoring in the off-season, and you have to re-hab them.

We try not to overlook anything. We even check their teeth for neglect and other problems. A lot of pain and sickness can be caused by dental infections.

No matter how hard they've worked, though, the players are still going to have some aches and pains, your basic blisters, minor stuff. But you don't see guys running wind sprints in rubber jackets or pounding fifteen salt pills like they used to. They're ready.

Q. What about the fabled attributes of Arizona's desert air?
A. *(Laughing.)* You won't believe it, but allergies are really a problem out here. Years ago, Arizona was where you sent people with allergies, but now the air is full of ragweed and olive and an abundance of dust. There's a million manmade lakes too, and everybody's got a pool. The first week of spring training, I've got players who feel drowsy or feel like they're getting sick, but it's allergies. Next to our orthopedist, the allergist is the busiest guy in camp.

window for pick-up starting three weeks before first game. Tickets also available through Dillard's Ticket Outlet, (602) 829-5151.

Autograph Opportunities: Excellent. Players returning from the practice fields share the sidewalk with fans and sometimes use the stadium steps to get to the field. "The Brewers are really good signers," says collector Mike Fox of Minneapolis. "I got autographs from guys walking right past the concession stands."

Says Mesa's Joe Miller, "There was a rumor that Gary Sheffield wasn't going to sign last spring because Uncle Dwight (Gooden) told him he could get paid for it. But Sheffield was pretty good."

Bob Uecker wasn't "cool" about signing, says collector Jeff Ashworth. "I was kind of disappointed that he didn't act like he does on TV."

Team Hotel: The Dobson Ranch Inn, 1666 South Dobson Road, Mesa, AZ 85202; (602) 831-7000. Milwaukeeans also stay at the Chandler Inn, the Lexington Suites, and the upscale San Marcos Hotel.

Nothing fancy about it, but you talk about your authentic Mexican food. It's the best."

Brewers public relations director Tom Skibosh makes several pilgrimages every spring to the China Gate in Mesa for something called "the Beggar's Pot." "It's a combination of lobster, shrimp, scallops, what-have-you—not deep-fried—and vegetables, and I love it. Their cashew chicken is also excellent."

Another Brewers favorite is the American Grill on Alma School Road, where the clam chowder is served in hollowed-out shepherd's bread. Other good bets for Brewer-watching include Harry & Steve's (in Scottsdale and Mesa), co-owned by former Cy Young–winning pitcher Steve Stone and Hall of Fame mouth Harry Caray; the Lunt Avenue Marble Club; and Tomoso's Italian restaurant.

Don't look for "Mr. Baseball," Bob Uecker, at any of them. "I don't go too many places anymore," says the Brewers broadcaster. "When I'm in Chandler, I just go to the ballpark. That's plenty for me."

Sounds like a man who's been locked out one time too many. ("Wow, they're having a good time in there!")

Area Attractions

• Golf at the **Ocotillo Golf Course,** near the stadium. The Brewers get free passes, so this is a good place to see ballplayers out of uniform and out of synch.

Restaurants, Lounges, and Dives: Brewers trainer John Adam (see sidebar), a former Scottsdale resident, says, "I'm half-Mexican, so I like the Mexican food places. There's a great hole-in-the-wall place in Chandler called Guedo's (pronounced WAY-doas, meaning "fair-complected male"). If you're a Chandler native, you know it.

Chamber of Commerce: 218 N. Arizona Ave., Chandler, AZ 85224; (602) 963-4571.

Spring Training Sites: 1971–72, Tempe, AZ; 1973–85, Sun City, AZ; 1986–present, Chandler.

Won–Lost Record/Attendance:

Year	Record	Attendance
1989	15–18	102,814
1988	15–17	83,706
1987	16–17	69,158
1986	16–12	50,344
1985	17–15	37,095

Home Of The
CLEVELAND
INDIANS
Tucson
Home of the Toros
ni corbett
TICKETS
1
2
3
4

STADIUM INFORMATION

Hi Corbett Field
Randolph Park
Tucson, AZ 85726
(602) 881-5710

How long at present location: Forty-four years
Capacity: 9,200
Dimensions: 366 feet to left, 392 feet to center, 348 feet to right
Directions: From I-10, exit on Broadway, go east to Randolph Way, turn right. Ballpark is on right side.
Parking: Paved, but inadequate, free. Spillover parking at adjacent golf course and nearby shopping mall.

If any ballpark is an antidote to those sterile new complexes springing up in Florida, it is Tucson's Hi Corbett Field. In honor of the regular tenant, the triple-A Tucson Toros (a Houston Astros farm club), the stadium is painted in bullfight colors—red, yellow, and blue. A fiesta atmosphere prevails in the gaily decorated concourses. Whimsical architectural flourishes, such as the baseball finials on the ticket-gate columns, are reminiscent of Dodgertown, but with a Mexican flair. Inside, the eye is treated to double- and even triple-tiered advertising on the outfield walls, a veritable riot of color and bold graphics.

Hi Corbett is surprisingly intimate for a stadium seating 9,200, thanks to its miserly foul territory, high walls, and eccentric dimensions (392 feet to center, but 410 feet to left-center and 405 feet to right-center). Two large areas along the first-base line are designated no-smoking and no-drinking sections.

Tucson is not the most convenient site for a spring-training camp because of the long bus rides to the other Cactus League parks, but the players praise it as a cosmopolitan city with a laid-back lifestyle and plenty of recreational opportunities. (In 1988, the Indians shared the local sports pages with the top-ranked University of Arizona basketball team, the NCAA regional basketball tournament at the University of Arizona's McKale Center, and the LPGA's Tucson Open golf championship at the Reid Park Golf Course, next to the ballpark.) They also appreciate the convenience of the minor-league facility, which is right behind the outfield wall.

Take your sunglasses, though. On March afternoons, the sun is high in the sky and in the face of the fans.

Ticket Information: box seats $5; reserved grandstand $4; unreserved grandstand $3.50; general admission (senior/military) $2; general admission (children fourteen and under) $1 (1990 prices). Season and single-game tickets available March 1 by mail (Hi Corbett Field, P.O. Box 27577, Tucson, AZ 85726) or phone, (602) 791-4266. Charge by phone: (602) 791-4836.

Autograph Opportunities: "It's good if you want Indians players," says Darren Russ of Baseball Cards, Etc. of Tucson, "but we sort of get the short end of the stick from visiting teams. The star players don't always come down from Phoenix because they don't want to make the long bus trip. Most of the Indians are real nice, though. I don't know of any who are real sticklers. There's a lot of security along the baselines and near the dugout where kids want to get signatures; they're strict about that. Otherwise, the access is very good."

"The people who go down to Tucson tell me they have great experiences," says Joe Miller of Mesa's Sports America. "They say they get their fill in a day."

Team Hotel: Viscount Suites, 4855 East Broadway, Tucson, AZ 85711; (602) 745-6500. None of the visiting teams stay in Tucson, preferring to drive back to their established digs.

Area Attractions

• **Old Tucson,** 201 South Kinney Road. This Old West town/soundstage/theme park was built in 1939 for the movie *Arizona* and has been used for countless television shows and more than a hundred feature films, including *Rio Lobo, The Outlaw Josey Wales,* and *Shootout at the OK Corral.* Open daily 9:00 A.M. to 5:00 P.M.

• **The Arizona-Sonora Desert Museum** in Tucson Mountain Park, fourteen miles west of downtown. More than 200 different animals and 400 kinds of plants in naturalistic desert settings. Called "the most distinctive zoo in the United States" by the *New York Times.* Open daily 8:30 A.M. to 5:00 P.M. in the spring (the animals are most active in the morning). Adults $6; children six to twelve $1; children under six free. 2021 North Kinney Road.

• **The Triple C Chuckwagon Suppers,** featuring The Sons of the Pioneers—sort of a sagebrush dinner theater with songs like "Cool Water" and "Tumbling Tumbleweeds" wrapped around a rustic indoor meal of beef, biscuits, and baked beans. Dinner and show, Tuesday-Saturday; Adults $15; children $10. 8900 Bopp Road, Tucson. Reservations: (602) 883-2333.

Restaurants, Lounges, and Dives: TGI Friday's is the premier hangout because it's right across the street from the team hotel. For prime rib and steaks, just about everyone goes to El Corral, but Gus & Andy's is a favorite of Herb Score, the Indians broadcaster. For seafood, it's the Solarium. "There's a Mexican place called Rosita's," says media relations director Rick Minch, "a little place you wouldn't know about unless somebody told you. It has excellent cheese crisps."

Feeling adventurous? "There's a strange place twenty miles or so out in the desert called L'il Abner's," says Sheldon Ocker, who covers the Indians for the *Akron Beacon Journal.* "It's on a dirt road, and it looks like some guy just built a shack out there. You've got to drive over the rattlesnakes to get to it, but the food is good. You eat outdoors if you want, and you can carve your name in the table with a knife." Says Indians traveling secretary Mike Seghi, "I like L'il Abner's even better than El Corral. It's like a stagecoach stop, and they serve ribs as big as dinosaur bones."

"Tucson has the best Mexican food in the world," says film producer Chris Chesser (see sidebar), "and I've lived in Mexico. It's that Sonoran-Mexican food that I grew up with. There's a place called La Fuenta, a great place for snowbirds and people from out of town because every night they have a floor show with a mariachi band. I was a waiter there once. Sometimes these crazy movie people would come in, and we'd say, 'What planet are they from?' Go to La Fuenta for mariachis and lots of Mexican pizzazz.

"Then there's the Molinas, who are sort of an extended family with restaurants in Tucson. The most popular is Casa Molina, but another one is El Molinito. That's probably my favorite restau-

> "The mostly cloudless or 'high' Arizona skies pose yet another problem for the players in that fly balls, even pop-ups, can simply disappear overhead, where there are no dark clouds to frame the ball. 'I just lost it' may be a lame excuse elsewhere, but in Arizona it is a perfectly acceptable alibi. The pursuit of the invisible ball is often, for fans at least, the source of high comedy, a scene out of *Topper.* Outfielders renowned for their sure fielding touch may be seen standing with faces turned helplessly upward, gloved hand waving to fend off the unseen, eyes blindly searching the stratosphere as the ball descends untouched only a few feet away. Even Willie Mays had days there when he looked like Lucy Van Pelt."
>
> —Ron Fimrite

rant. It's a converted fast-food place on 22nd Street. You order at a counter. They make the flour tortillas and the corn chips for the other restaurants. The best Mexican food I've had."

For ice cream, the Indians press corps suggests Eric's Ice Cream (Campbell & Speedway), on the edge of the UA campus. Specialty: mix-ins.

Chamber of Commerce: P.O. Box 991, Tucson, AZ 85701; (602) 792-2250.

Spring Training Sites: 1902–03, New Orleans; 1904, San Antonio, TX; 1905–06, New Orleans; 1907–09, Macon, GA; 1910–11, Alexandria, LA; 1912, New Orleans; 1913, Pensacola, FL; 1914, Athens, GA; 1915, San Antonio, TX; 1916–20, New Orleans; 1921–22, Dallas; 1923–27, Lakeland, FL; 1928–39, New Orleans; 1940–42, Fort Myers, FL; 1943–45, Lafayette, IN; 1946, Clearwater, FL; 1947–present, Tucson.

Won-Lost Record/Attendance:

Year	Record	Attendance
1989	19–11–1	68,850
1988	18–13	65,441
1987	13–15–1	61,595
1986	14–16	46,481
1985	12–16	53,574

The Man Who Made a Movie Star of Hi Corbett Field

Chris Chesser, who produced the 1989 Paramount release *Major League,* grew up a few blocks from Hi Corbett Field, the Cleveland Indians' spring-training facility. The Tucson ballpark provided the landscape for most of the film's early scenes. Moreover, the team in the movie, although fictional, is the Cleveland Indians. So, the first question out of the interviewer's mouth was, naturally . . .

Q: You must be a big Indians fan.
Chesser: No, I'm a huge Yankees fan. I much prefer going to Anaheim for a game, even though I live fifteen minutes from Dodger Stadium, because I've always been a junior circuit kind of guy. When I was a kid, the "Game of the Week" was always the Yankees against somebody, and I was a big Mickey Mantle fan. Believe me, it was odd making a film in which my club was the villain.

Q: Did you spend a lot of time at Hi Corbett Field as a youngster?
A: Oh, yes. We moved to Tucson in 1949, and I lived there till I went away to college, so I was there during the fifties. I never sold drinks at Hi

DOBSON
RANCH
INN

Corbett, but I chased balls a ton. I remember the older players—Jimmy Piersall, Leon Wagner, Rocky Colovito, Sudden Sam McDowell. Indians kind of guys. There's a civic group called the El Conquistadors that sponsored stuff, and I remember going to little parties and meeting retired guys like Bob Lemon, Joe Gordon, Lou Boudreau. People would say to me, "That's Joe Gordon!" He just looked like an old guy to me, but I remember how nice those guys were to me, too.

Q: Aside from sentimental reasons, why did you film parts of *Major League* in Tucson?
A: That's because of David Ward. When I stopped being a studio guy in the early eighties, my approach was to strike up relationships with writer-directors whose work I admired. David Ward was one of the first I approached, because I thought his *Cannery Row* was one of the best scripts I'd read. It turned out David was a huge sports fan. He was raised in Cleveland, and he really wanted to do a story about the Cleveland Indians, an underdog team, because they were perennial losers of a magnitude people didn't even appreciate. I mean, they haven't won a pennant since 1954, a World Series since 1948.

So we got a studio to develop it. It took five or six years to get the picture financed. When we finally got into pre-production and asked, "Where do we shoot this?" the logical places were Tucson and Cleveland. As it turned out, most of the picture was shot in Milwaukee because of scheduling problems in Cleveland, but there was no reason not to do it in Tucson. It was convenient, just an hour's plane flight out of L.A.

Q: You filmed in Tucson . . . in July?
A: Yeah, it was July of 1988. We shot all day long, and it was easily over a hundred every day, averaged a hundred and five. It was also monsoon time there; we got a little rain. We shot some of that stuff under pretty cloudy skies.

Q: Corbin Bernsen, Charlie Sheen, and Tom Berenger—you came up with three leading men who look plausible in baseball uniforms . . . Indians uniforms, anyway.
A: Before we even got to Tucson, we hired (former Dodgers catcher) Steve Yeager as technical consultant. He worked with Tom and Charlie for a week at Tom's home in North Carolina. They just went down there and played ball. Charlie already was a real good ballplayer, so Steve just worked with his mechanics and his release point. Tom, on the other hand, was a good athlete, a football player, but he was not a baseball catcher. With him it was more basic, learning what catchers do, the raw stuff first and then the subtleties.

Steve also helped with our casting of the other parts by running a minicamp in L.A. in June. Specifically, we had to fill the parts of Pedro Cerrano, the Caribbean slugger; Roger Dorn, the third baseman; and Willie Mays Hays, the speedster. We read a lot of guys for those three parts. We just saw hundreds of guys. We'd read them, then either David Ward or I would take them outside and play catch with them. We had to, because if you ask an actor if he can ride a horse, it's always, "Can *I* ride a *horse?* Why, I was junior rodeo champion . . ." We literally had guys who said they were triple-A players, and when we went out with them they couldn't even throw.

Anyway, we rated the guys according to how they played catch. When we got down to some final candidates for those parts, we had a tryout day at a park in Beverly Hills and played ball for three or four hours. Yeager would hit fungoes, we'd pitch to them to see how they could hit. Wesley Snipes got the role of Willie Mays Hays. It wasn't important that he actually be fast, but he had to look fast. In fact, he was an incredible athlete. That slow-motion catch over the wall that he does at the end of the movie? He did that, it wasn't a double. And Dennis Haysbert, the actor who played Cerrano? In the scene where he was supposed to hit the ball out of the

9

park, he actually hit the ball out of the park! Yeager did a great job for us.

But we still didn't have a Dorn, and we didn't have anybody to play the aging relief pitcher. We read Chelsie Ross in Chicago, he got the pitcher's role. He actually was a semi-pro pitcher and played college ball in Texas.

Still no Dorn.

Yeager met us in Tucson for another tryout, this time to find kids to play the other ballplayers in the movie. We got a hefty list of ex–University of Arizona players, and we went out early one morning to hit balls at 'em and let 'em bat. The best ones we hired. Then the minicamp began in earnest. It took a week of workouts, a couple of times a day, to get everybody's chops up again.

Q: Still no Dorn?
A: We finally closed Corbin, but he didn't show until two or three days before shooting. He had pretty long hair because he was doing another picture, and he couldn't cut it because he still had a couple of scenes to do back in L.A. The first couple of days, we had to pin all his hair back and stick it up under his hat. The scene where he complains to the manager and the manager pisses on his contract, he had long hair under his hat for that.

Q: Did anybody get hurt during the shooting?
A: We didn't have too many scares. Wesley was working with Yeager on his head-first slides, trying to look like Rickey Henderson, and he jammed his wrist in that scene where he slides into second base and doesn't make it to the bag. I took him to the doctor, but it was fine in three or four days. Nobody got hit by a line drive, thank goodness. Charlie's arm was sore for a couple of days, and that was scary because it was an insurance thing, but he was okay.

We did have some scary stuff. There's a slow-mo sequence where Tom Berenger, playing Jake Taylor, gets run over at the plate on a throw from the relay guy and gets knocked about ten feet. There's a cute little bit where he gets up holding the ball and heads for the wrong dugout, dazed. We decided to use a real catcher rather than a stunt man, and a couple of guys volunteered. We needed two guys, a base runner and the double. Well, the whack that we used in the film, the kid really did get hit, and he got hit hard like that two or three times. As big as those hits were, though, nobody got hurt, but it was a real concern.

Q: There's a scene in spring training where Corbin Bernsen won't dive for ground balls. There's a scene later where he's practicing hard and taking balls off his chest in fielding practice.
A: We did both of those the same day. Some were hit to him and some were thrown. Where he's not trying hard, those are real baseballs. The ones off his chest, those are softer baseballs.

Q: Which of your stars was the best ballplayer?
A: That's pretty sensitive, because Tom, although a very good athlete, was not a good baseball player. It's a tribute to Tom as an actor that he made things look good on screen. We didn't have to double him a lot. He caught great, you didn't have to throw soft to him. He really caught Charlie when Charlie was throwing hard. It was the other things, the throw to second, the footwork, that he had trouble with.

There was no problem with Charlie, cause he really does have a mid-eighties heater and could probably have played some pro ball. Corbin played a lot of organized ball as a kid, and he plays in celebrity games in L.A. So, in answer to your question: Charlie was real good, Corbin was fine, and Tom was a heck of an actor.

Q: There's a spring-training scene where the players show up and walk into a room that looks like an Army barracks. Shouldn't the players have been staying in condos, like real major-leaguers?
A: That's a case where a story point got cut. We wanted to establish that the Indians were in fi-

nancial trouble, and there was stuff we shot that would have made that clear. There was a sequence when Tom first gets there. He goes into the bunkhouse with Yeager, who played the third-base coach. They walk in together, he looks around and says to Yeager, "What happened to where we normally stay?" And Boomer's response is, "Austerity measures, buddy. This is what happens when you finish twenty games out." That interior barracks stuff was shot weeks later in Milwaukee. We actually shot it in a jail, a prison lockup facility. People actually lived in that room, and they came back to it every night.

Q: Hi Corbett Field is a pretty photogenic ballpark.
A: It is, and it was painful to us not to establish Hi Corbett any better than we did. We wanted to shoot from the outfield to show those stands with the Catalina Mountains behind it. Unfortunately, photographing baseball is very laborious. It happens over long distances, and the only way to make it believable—and verisimilitude is the most important thing—is to shoot most of the baseball action with a lot of cuts instead of long shots. We shot with a lot of setups, a minimum of twenty or thirty a day. The simplest scene required three or four. Move the camera, relight. As a consequence, we weren't able to establish more of the park and the mountains, to contrast with Cleveland later.

In terms of the look of the park, you'll remember our first look at Hi Corbett—the camera pans over cactus and rocks, there's a Gila monster on the rock. Obviously, those things weren't there. We shot that in the middle of the parking lot, and we had to move in that landscape. My brother Steve is a landscaper in Tucson specializing in desert landscapes. He did a great job for us.

Q: All in all, it's a case of hometown boy putting the hometown ballpark on the map.
A: Yeah. It's funny, when I was a little kid, I got mad at Mom and Dad once—they'd given me too much yard work or something—and I ran away from home. I only got as far as Hi Corbett, maybe five or six blocks. I hid in a culvert under the street for five or six hours.

Q: That makes you the Phantom of Hi Corbett Field.
A: Maybe so. Is there a movie idea there?

59¢
TACO B
CARTE
30

STADIUM INFORMATION

Desert Sun Stadium
Ray A. Kroc Baseball Complex
Avenue A at 35th Street
Yuma, AZ 85346
(602) 726-6040

How long at present location: Twenty-two years
Capacity: 6,784
Dimensions: 350 feet down lines, 385 feet alleys, 420 feet to center
Directions: From I-8, take 16th Street west to Avenue A; turn left and follow for two miles. Ballpark is on right. From Phoenix, take Route 10 to Buckeye; go south on 85; take Highway 8 W; take 32nd St. West exit, follow to Avenue A and turn left. Ballpark is on right.
Alternate directions: If you're walking or running, Anna Teter, former president of the San Diego Madres fan club (see sidebar), suggests starting at Jack Murphy Stadium in San Diego. Take Friar's Road to Mission Gorge, then up Zion to Waring, then onto Navajo Road to Fletcher Parkway, then down Johnson to Main Street in El Cajon; take Granite Hills Road, which runs into Dehesa Road. ("Now you're out into the far reaches of the county.") Continue past Pine Valley, climb over the mountains, and get on Old Highway 80 paralleling I-8. From there, it's just a seventy-mile walk across the desert to Yuma. "Look for the Yuma water tower," Ms. Teter says. "The stadium's right there."
Parking: Dusty, but plentiful.

Yuma is bleached-bones baseball. This cavalry camp of a training site wouldn't know what shade was if it weren't for the long shadow of the Yuma water tower. Gila monsters have been known to pass by without a backward glance. Clouds of dust and cars crunching on gravel greet you on arrival, with overflights of military helicopters and jet fighters thrown in to seal the impression that you've bought a seat at Ground Zero and it's blast day. This is the farthest outpost of spring baseball, the last place a big-city fan would ever visit. If you've been to Yuma, you are truly a spring-training fanatic.

Unless you're from San Diego. Then you're just a fan with a car and a few hours to kill.

The beauty of Yuma is that it's just three hours from San Diego by car, making it easy for Padres fans to take in a ballgame, top off the gas tank, and still get back to Oz before the zoo closes. According to club officials, about ninety percent of the Padres' spring-training tickets are sold right in San Diego.

Yuma's remoteness, however, forces the Padres to leave their camp for long stretches in search of Cactus League opponents. Typically, they park in Scottsdale for a week or two to play the Phoenix teams and sleep on clean sheets; then they return to Yuma for a long home stand. The heel of the exhibition season is spent wandering around the California and Nevada deserts looking for a game. Beautiful San Diego, when it finally comes into view, resembles a mirage.

Rainouts are unheard of, but take an umbrella anyway. For the sun.

Ticket Information: reserved grandstand $5; bleachers $4 (1990 prices). General admission tickets on sale three hours prior to game. For tickets, write Caballeros de Yuma, P.O. Box 230, Yuma, AZ 85364. No phone orders, but call (602) 782-2567 for information.

Autograph Opportunities: A company of autographs hounds rode out there a month ago, but they haven't been heard from since. Buzzards probably got 'em.

Team Hotel: Park Inn International, 2600 S. 4th Ave., Yuma, AZ 85364; (602) 726-4830. The Fourth Avenue strip of motels also includes the Chilton Inn and Conference Center. The Stardust Resort Hotel, where the Cubs used to bunk, alas, is no more. Farewell to the palm-sheltered swimming pool, "Roman Hot Plunge," and fifties-style motel architecture.

Area Attractions

• **Yakult Swallows** spring-training. The Japanese baseball team works out and plays intersquad games at the Kroc complex from late January to March 1.

• Sand dunes in the Great American Sahara Desert, fifteen miles west of Tucson on I-8. "They've made a lot of motion pictures out there," says Ida Scott of the Yuma Chamber of Commerce, remembering, no doubt, Sly Stallone staggering around with needle eyes and swollen tongue. The dunes are a popular playground for dune buggies and all-terrain vehicles, but California law requires seat belts and helmets for all riders and passengers. There are no ATVs to rent. "Bring your own," says Ms. Scott.

Restaurants, Lounges, and Dives: Padres public relations director Bill Beck says, "There's not a lot to do in Yuma, but there's some good restaurants, and what the hell do you do in spring-training anyway except go out and eat?" Beck recommends the Chinese food at the Mandarin Palace on 32nd St. ("As good as I've had anyplace.")

John Maffei of the *North County Blade Tribune:* "If you like steak, there's a good steak house called Jack & Rosie's in the old part of town. It's an old restaurant where all the waitresses are sixty-five and call you 'Dearie,' but the food's really good. And there's a Mexican restaurant I like called Cretin's right near Jack & Rosie's. You go in and it's like a Marines museum—autograph pictures of generals, that sort of thing. Eisenhower's been there, Omar Bradley. Every famous commander in the Marines seems to have eaten at Cretin's. It's not an attractive building, it's like an old dance hall, but the food is very good."

"Most of the players hang out at the Shiloh Inn," says Bob Nightengale, who covers the Padres for the Los Angeles Times. "There's a small dance floor, but mostly it's a place to drink. It's the in spot for the twenty-five-to-forty crowd."

Chamber of Commerce: 377 S. Main St., Yuma, AZ 85364; (602) 782-2567.

Spring Training Sites: 1969–present, Yuma.

Won-Lost Record/Attendance:

Year	Record	Attendance
1989	18–8–1	69,541
1988	11–16	59,485
1987	13–16	59,531
1986	16–14	62,103
1985	11–15–1	53,167

WHITSO
31

The Loneliness of the Long-distance Padres Fan

Anna Teter, thirty-one and unmarried, works for the San Diego Unified School District as an interpreter for deaf and hard-of-hearing students. In her less-rational hours, she is a member (and past president) of the San Diego Madres, a 480-woman fan club that supports the Padres and raises money for thirty-eight Little League teams. In her even-less-rational hours, she runs long distances. Two springs ago, she ran all the way from San Diego's Jack Murphy Stadium to Yuma's Desert Sun Stadium—189 miles of urban sprawl, mountains, and searing desert—just to see a Padres game.

The run took six days. Next time, she says, she'll do it in five.

Q: Why?
A: I've always liked long-distance running. And I've always liked baseball. My family lived on a hill near Jack Murphy Stadium, and I used to run there with my dad. We'd go to the parking lot and run circles around the stadium.

Anyway, a few years I read about two Padre rookies who ran to Yuma. It took them two weeks. I said, "I can do that. If it took them two weeks, I can do it in seven days."

Q: Who were the two rookies?
A: No one remembers! They got cut. It was back in, like, 1982, and everyone vaguely remembers it, but no one can tell me who they were or what route they took.

Anyway, I wanted to run to Yuma. I set it all up years ago. I talked to CalTrans, they okayed it and gave me routes . . . because there are certain areas where you have to run on the freeway. But I put it off. Finally, I said, "This is a good time, I'm in shape, I might as well do it."

Q: Was it an ordeal?
A: Not really. It sounds impressive, but it wasn't. I wanted that big physiological challenge, but the first couple of days I felt I wasn't suffering enough physiologically! *(Laughs)* By the third day, though, my knees felt like someone had been beating on them with a hammer. My right knee started hurting first because of the curvature of the road. The pain was like bone hitting bone, and I was tempted to quit. But by then, too many people had heard about it, and I felt I had to keep going for the Madres. People think we're just a bunch of little old ladies, and I've tried for years to dispel that myth.

The first three days were also hard because we had to drive back each night to San Diego. I had read this book about the man who ran across America—he was my model—and he stayed at motels along the way. I couldn't afford that, so I was dependent on my road crew to drive me to my drop-off point and get me back at night. The next two nights I stayed in El Centro.

Q: How far was it to the mountains?
A: It's about eighty-nine miles. Jacumba is the last big city before you hit the mountains—I don't know what they're called—and the mountain part is about eleven miles. Once I got over the mountain part into the Ocotillo area, the sand was wonderful. The other side of the mountains, the traffic is nothing, I could criss-cross the highway.

Q: How were you dressed for this?
A: Shorts. I'd start off in the morning with a T-shirt, and then a tank top as it warmed up. Visor. Lots of sunscreen. The first day, I miscalculated and ended up with this truck-driver sunburn.

Q: Were you still running on highways?
A: From the mountains to Yuma, I took basically old Highway 80, which parallels Interstate 8. Past the mountains there's a stretch where I

had permission from the Highway Patrol to run on the freeway. Sure enough, I'm running on the freeway and all these police cars go by. No big deal. I've got a mile and a half to go when the air patrol comes by. The plane starts buzzing me, and a loudspeaker is going, "Get off the freeway! Get off the freeway!" Well, I had just been to traffic school for getting a ticket, and I didn't want to get another, so I had to get off the freeway. That was frustrating.

Q: Was the desert difficult?
A: I thought it might get boring, but it never did. It does get psychologically depressing, though, because it's seventy miles and it's flat and you don't see anything for a while. I had a radio and a water bottle. You dry out real fast. I carried water, and in ten minutes I'd be out.

The first day on the desert, it was really windy. I listened to the Padres game on headphones, and they almost cancelled the game because of the wind. Fortunately, it was at my back.

I thought I'd see a lot of wildlife, even dead animals, but I didn't see anything. I did see some Brahma cows, and I yelled "Hi." They came up to the fence to be petted. I stopped and got pictures of me petting these cows like a bunch of puppies.

It was hard when I got close to Yuma. It was only five hours of running, but I didn't want to arrive at night, so I had to stop. By that time, I felt the run had been dragged out too long anyway.

Q: How were you received in Yuma?
A: Well, I visualized running into the stadium with all the people cheering, like with a marathon. I love that. But I had to start a day late, and Thursday's was a night game. Anyway, KFMB radio wanted me to come in while they were on the air, but I got there an hour early by accident—I forgot there's an hour's time difference! The teams were working out, and they had the gate open, and I thought, "Hey, I'm not gonna go back and run in again an hour from now." So I ran around the whole complex and then ran onto the field. It's great to run into a stadium—even if it's Yuma's stadium.

Q: Who won the game?
A: The Padres. It went extra innings. I had ice on my knees—beer cans, actually. Jerry Coleman, the radio announcer, said come on up, but I just couldn't walk up the stairs, I was so sore.

I'm glad I did it, though, it was fun.

Q: Any final thoughts?
A: Nature is beautiful and wonderful and all that, but next time I hope I can talk somebody into running with me.

PALM SPRINGS
Angels
ANGELS STADIUM
SPRING HOME

STADIUM INFORMATION

Gene Autry Park
4125 East McKellips
Mesa, AZ 85205
(602) 830-4137

Angels Stadium
Sunrise Way at Baristo Road
Palm Springs, CA 92263
P.O. Box 609
(619) 327-1266

How long at present location: Twenty-nine years
Capacity (Angels Stadium): 6,371
Dimensions: 360 feet down lines, 400 feet to center
Directions: To Gene Autry Park, take I-10 to Superstition Freeway (360 East), exit Superstition at Mesa Drive, turn left; turn right on McKellips and follow to Gene Autry Park. To Angels Stadium, exit I-10 at Gene Autry Drive, head south to Ramon and turn right; turn right again at Sunrise, and then right again on Baristo Road. From North Palm Canyon Drive (Highway 111), take Ramon Road east to Sunrise and turn left; right at Baristo.
Parking: Stadium parking is limited, but street parking and nearby lots handle spillover. The neighborhood is nice, making for a pleasant walk, and kids can run around in the park before the game.

By some lucky happenstance, the Angels' two-week home stand roughly coincides with the annual descent upon Palm Springs of thousands of cheerful, beer-breathed, water-gun assassins on furlough from college. While Fort Lauderdale has taken steps to diminish its annual bacchanal, Palm Springs is trying to control and redirect the energies of its spring-breakers (in the manner of nuclear engineers inserting and withdrawing fuel rods from a glowing nuclear pile). One local newspaper follows these efforts with a front-page box that reads like this:

"SPRING BREAK—Today's Weather: Sunny, with winds to 25 mph. Highs in the upper 70s to mid-80s. Lows in the 50s. Monday Arrests: 198. Total Arrests: 388. Monday Driving Time at 8 P.M. (time to get from Vista Chino to Ramon Road on Palm Canyon Drive): 21 minutes (normal: 7 minutes)."

Surprisingly, the spring baseball experience is almost untouched by the student high jinks. Angels Stadium is in a lovely park not far from Palm Canyon Drive, and there are few prettier places to watch a ballgame. Tall palm trees and the looming curtain of the San Jacinto Mountains compete with baseball for the eye, and it's easy to drift off into spring reveries between cracks of the bat.

This is a small, intimate ballpark, and home plate is very close to the stands. The unfortunate trade-off for this closeness is that safety screens force almost everybody to watch the game through 9-gauge wire. The wily fan will avoid sitting higher than the fourth row behind home plate; a sloping, trapeze-style net interferes with the view.

A few more spring-break pointers:

- Most of the action is at night and centers on

Spring breakers on Palm Canyon Drive

Palm Canyon Drive. The police barricade most of the cross streets between Palm Canyon and Indian Avenue (both one-way streets), creating a huge loop for the kids to cruise in their motorized boom-boxes. From the sidewalks, the resulting crawl of convertibles and customized vans is better than the Parade of Roses.

• If you have a son or daughter in college, stay away. You won't sleep well, knowing what goes on here.

• Above all, avoid budget motels during the infestation. Dante would have rewritten his *Inferno* if he'd spent just one night in a thin-walled motel full of shrieking, thumping spring-breakers.

Ticket Information: At press time, the Angels had not yet released their 1991 ticket prices. Last year's prices were box $5; general admission $4. For current ticket information, call (714) 937-6700.

Autograph Opportunities: At Palm Springs, the pickings are poor—screens and netting separate the fans and players. What's worse, a below-grade trench under the grandstand permits players and coaches to watch the game and visit the clubhouse with no danger of exposure to fans.

Mesa, Arizona, is another story. Gene Autry Park, where the Angels work out for the first month of spring-training—they have no "home" games until the last two weeks—is wide open to fans and autograph hunters.

"The best time to get autographs is the first week and a half of spring-training, before the games start," says collector Joe Miller of Mesa. "Go in the morning, when the players are arriving. Wally Joyner's a tough autograph; he'll sign three or four and that's it. But Jim Abbot will stay out there all day until the kids are taken care of."

Angels public relations director Tim Mead says: "Players, for the most part, don't mind signing things, but what they don't like is when a kid shoves five cards at them to sign. It's better to have one important item you want signed."

Team Hotel: In Mesa, the Rodeway Inn, 5700 East Main Street, Mesa, AZ 85205; (602) 985-3561. Also the Hilton Inn, 1011 West Holmes Avenue, Mesa, AZ 85210; (602) 833-5555. In Palm Springs, the team hotel is—what else?—the Gene Autry Hotel, 4200 East Palm Canyon Drive, Palm Springs, CA 92264; (619) 328-1171. Numerous other hotels are close to Angels Stadium, from modest motels to pricey resorts.

Area Attractions

• **Golf.** Dozens of public courses and golf resorts dot the desert from Palm Springs to La Quinta, some of them familiar to viewers of televised PGA events. For a visitor's guide to golf in the area, write the Palm Springs Desert Resort Convention and Visitors Bureau (address below).
• Polo at the **Eldorado Polo Club,** Indio, "the winter polo capital of the West." Admission $5.
• **Ice Capades Chalet** at Palm Desert Town Center. A 160-foot ice-skating rink with full-time disc jockey, group classes, and visits by former and current Ice Capades stars. Admission is $4, seniors $2.50, skate rental $1.50.
• **Oasis Water Resort**, a twenty-one acre water recreation park, features a 29,000-square-foot wave pool and a 500-foot whitewater "river." Admission is $12.95, seniors and kids four to eleven $9.95. 1500 Gene Autry Trail.
• The **Aerial Tramway** on Tramway Drive, Chino Canyon off Highway 111 (north). Billed as "the world's most spectacular aerial ride," the tramway's mountain station at 8,516 feet features a restaurant, lounge, gift shop, picnic area, and fifty-four miles of hiking trails. Open 10:00 A.M. weekdays, 8:00 A.M. weekends, mid-October through April. Adults $12.95; children under thirteen $7.95.
• **Art galleries.** Too numerous to mention. Check *Travelhost* magazine or the visitor's guide for current exhibitions.
• **Palm Springs Desert Museum,** a privately funded art and natural science museum. Desert Fashion Plaza at 101 Museum Drive. Call (619) 325-7186 for hours and admission fees.
• **Living Desert**, a 1,200-acre "desert interpretive center" in Palm Desert, offers six miles of nature trails and desert exhibits. It's open daily, 9:00 A.M. to 5:00 P.M. Adults $3.50; children three to fifteen $1; children two and under free. Highway 111, Palm Desert.

Restaurants, Lounges, and Dives: "My old standby is Dominick's in Rancho Mirage," says Melvin Durslag of the *Los Angeles Herald-Examiner.* "It's Italian, it's got a chicken in the pot . . . it's just a fun place to go. Dominick is kind of a character; he's been around a long time. He's not gonna overwhelm you with gourmet food, but it's a lively place. It's Gene Mauch's favorite place, he lives there in Rancho Mirage. Gene and Jackie Autry go there, too. It's sort of the Matteo's of Palm Springs."

Mike Penner of the *Los Angeles Times* recommends Las Casuelas Terraza, a Mexican restaurant on Palm Canyon Drive. "A lot of writers hang out there, sit on the patio, and watch people walk by. The big things there are the chicken fajitas, and the margaritas are great." (There is also a Las Casuelas Nuevas on Highway 111 in Rancho Mirage.)

Bobby Brett, brother to George (and George's manager), touts the Chart House in Rancho Mirage: "It's a steak, fish, and salad bar kind of place built right into the side of a rock mountain. That's my favorite. Very good food, plus

ngels
21

they've got good-looking waitresses. We know 'em all and get a table right away."

As far as dives go, nothing beats Nonchalant's on Highway 111 in Palm Desert, a place touted by *Golf Digest* writer Dwayne Netland. This is where the silver-haired set tucks in its collective gut and pretends it's the fifties all over again. Great live music, flattering lighting, and a dance floor packed with wild, gyrating pseudo-teens. "Good bar food, too," says Netland.

Chamber of Commerce: Palm Springs Desert Resort Convention and Visitors Bureau, 255 North El Cielo Road, Suite 315, Palm Springs, CA 92262; (619) 327-8411.

Spring Training Sites: 1966–79, Holtville, CA; 1980–81, Palm Springs, CA; 1982–83, Casa Grande, CA; 1984–present, Mesa, AZ (Note: The Angels have always played their home games in Palm Springs; these are training sites only.)

Won–Lost Record/Attendance:

Year	Record	Attendance
1989	14–15	56,034
1988	15–14	58,847
1987	15–15	57,277
1986	15–14	53,158
1985	15–11	48,102

"After Christmas, when I was a boy, I used to cry sometimes. My mother would ask me why, and I'd tell her, 'Because it's a whole year till next Christmas.' And that's how I feel about spring-training. When it's over, I want to cry."

—Charlie Briley, owner of the Pink Pony